Happy birthday, Chris –
Louise

The Face of Friendship

Many, many for your birthday Chris,
blessings,
Roāine. Jerusalem, June 2004.

Love do you Chris
+ birthday blessings
xo Mary

Love + Prayers
Hazel

with love
Hilary

Love
+
hugs
to you
Marian xxx & Anne O.

HAPPY Belated
Birthday to
you. mey GOD Renew
you in his love
always.
Peace Jane

love,
Louise

Love
Shirley x.

Chris,
I'm so glad you
were born + I really TRUST
you'll LOVE this book!
I did. Love
always Sue M.

A very special
remembrance
Patric

June 8/09

Chris may your
Birthday we celebrated
again when you get home.
a great gift for L'Arche you are
So glad to have met you.
Peace, Joy, a Hug,
Evelyne

Chris, great to spend the
blessed time w/ you in Israel
+ to "sing" to you in person
grace See V.

The Face of Friendship

A True Story of Hope and Transformation

Bill Clarke, S.J.

*With a foreword by Jean Vanier
and letters from Louisa Blair*

NOVALIS

Cover design: Novalis
Cover image: Will Croker/Getty Images
Layout: Richard Proulx

Business Office:
Novalis
49 Front Street East, 2nd Floor
Toronto, Ontario, Canada
M5E 1B3

Phone: 1-800-702-7773 or (416) 363-3303
Fax: 1-877-702-7775 or (416) 363-9409
E-mail: cservice@novalis.ca
www.novalis.ca

National Library of Canada Cataloguing in Publication

Clarke, Bill
    The face of friendship : a true story of hope and transformation / Bill Clarke ; with a foreword by Jean Vanier ; and letters from Louisa Blair.

ISBN 2-89507-485-2

    1. Ignatius Farm Community. 2. Jesuits—Ontario—Guelph Region. 3. Marginality, Social—Religious aspects—Catholic Church. 4. Clarke, Bill. 5. Dunn, Byron. I. Title.

BX2347.72.C3C54 2004   253'.088'2555300971343   C2004-900793-9

Printed in Canada.

We acknowledge the financial support of the Government of Canada through the Book Publishing Industry Development Program (BPIDP) for our publishing activities.

5 4 3 2 1   08 07 06 05 04

Contents

*For Byron
and all those who knew
and cared for him*

Foreword

Tears welled up in my eyes as I walked with Byron and Bill through their story. Tears began to flow as I came to the end of this book: Byron dying, transformed from a man of violence with an obsessive need for alcohol into a gentle, peaceful man ready to meet God who was already living in him, and Bill, continuing his journey, transformed more fully in the compassion of Jesus.

This is a story of covenant and friendship and gentle fidelity day after day, a story of playing cards, fishing, laughing, crying. It is also a story of despair and hope, of anger and forgiveness, which reveals to us the paschal mystery, the triumph of life over death.

This is not a book about ideas. It is neither a theological nor a spiritual discourse. This is a book about life, real life: life in this broken world of ours where each of us begins our journey in the womb of a woman and in a family. There we are gradually moulded into love and fear, into attitudes of hope and despair, into compassion for others or compulsions for power, success or alcohol.

Our world is like an immense gaping wound. Some people go through painful experiences and are placed in foster families or hospitals or prisons. Nobody ever asked them if they wanted to come into this world, where they wanted to live or with whom. Then they spend the rest of their lives trying to forget or ease the pain of not being appreciated and loved. Some drown their lives in alcohol. Others hide behind material success. Many drown themselves in work. Still others wander back and forth between success and desperation. The danger for some of us is to slip away in a spiritual journey of some kind, running away from the pain of reality. Many humbly try to cope and find their way, but they do not have the network of friends, the community, to give them the necessary support.

But all of us, at one moment or another, taste a moment of friendship, love and communion where hope is born in the womb of love. This book is about such a moment and its lifelong impact.

Yet hope and despair are so close one to another; they often go hand in hand. Some people discover, deeper than the wounds of the world or the wounds of their heart, a presence of God that gives meaning to all the pain and guides them along a journey of growth in trust. Again, this book describes such a life-changing discovery.

Bill tells us his own story, a story that is intimately bonded to Byron's story. It is a story of truth. He does not idealize or theorize but describes how we can all be healed and grow in inner peace, how our world can be healed. Bill and Byron's story is about bridging the gap between the so-called poor and weak and the so-called rich and strong, between the so-called successful and the so-called failures. But who is really poor and who is really rich? Who is really strong and who is really weak? Who is really a success and who is really a failure? As this book shows so poignantly, such things can easily be turned upside down.

Bill, the priest; Byron, the ex-convict. Byron gradually healing and freeing Bill, helping him to discover that we are all more or less "convicts," imprisoned in fear and waiting, yearning to be freed.

I have known Bill for 38 years now. We lived together in the community of l'Arche, in Trosly-Breuil, here in France, for two years. Since that time, we have been together in many different situations. I have visited his Farm community in Ontario and followed several retreats given by him. Bill Clarke is a beloved brother who has taught me so much and led me closer to Jesus.

Bill is a silent man, a listener more than a talker. Maybe that is what Jesus is like, a silent listener who loves you and me and wants to become our friend.

This is more than a book. It is a revelation of a "way," a way to truth and to peace. A way to compassion, which is at the heart of the message of Jesus. A way where we are healed by and through the poor and the rejected.

The Ignatius Farm Community where Bill and Byron lived and shared their lives with others had to close for reasons that Bill explains in this moving book. Perhaps such communities cannot last for a long time, but are called to be like beautiful flowers that blossom and then die, and that reveal the beauty of God and of the human heart.

Jean Vanier
L'Arche
Trosly-Breuil, France

Introduction

Like most stories, this one, which is about my journey with a man by the name of Byron Dunn, is part of a larger tale, so to set the context I have to begin with another story.

Two of us stood in the driveway of a nicely refurbished old home on a quiet residential street in the heart of Buffalo, New York. I was fighting back tears as I looked into the dark eyes of my friend Frank, eyes that as always vibrated back and forth nervously, our faces only a foot apart so that I was not too out of focus for his extreme short-sightedness. I struggled to find the appropriate words:

"Well, Frank, it has been a wonderful experience to live in community with you these past eight years. We have become good friends."

As usual, his response was honest and terse: "That's right." This simple acknowledgment of a relationship of true friendship was a precious gift to me and a tribute to how the eight years of living in community had opened up Frank's carefully guarded heart.

"I hope and pray that you will enjoy living here in your new home back here in your own country. I'm sure that you will be a blessing for the people here just as you have been a blessing in my life and in the lives of all the people you touched in the Farm Community."

"Yes."

"Anyway, my brother, we will always be friends, and we will certainly keep in touch. I'll give you a call in a couple of days."

"All right."

I managed to hold back the tears during our extended farewell hug, and until I had driven down the street and around the corner. Then, aware that I was heading back towards Guelph, Ontario, to what for the past 21 years had been my family, my home – Ignatius Farm Community, which by virtue of this final farewell was no more – the floodgates opened. I was reminded of another tearful, lonely drive back to the same Farm Community some years earlier after a more radical farewell to my friend Byron Dunn.

This community of welcome and support for men and women with various forms of disabilities, coming out of prison or psychiatric hospital or other situations of brokenness or alienation, was founded by a Jesuit, Fr. Doug McCarthy, and a married couple, Louise and Dick Anstett. At that time Doug was the chaplain at the local prison, the Guelph Correctional Institute, and Louise and Dick were his long-time friends. The vision for the community was that it would be a place of healing and growth for all its members living and working together on a farm, a community sustained more by friendship and faith than by formal structures. Any distinction between those who came as volunteer helpers and those who came out of deep need was to be minimized as far as possible. The community always remained very fragile and teetered on the edge of chaos, since at its heart were very vulnerable people whose lives were often filled with pain and chaos. However, this very fragility was part of the community's beauty and strength.

An article in the *Toronto Star* entitled "Paradise Lost" (May 20, 2001) expresses the significance of what was being lost by the impending closure:

> Members of the Ignatius Farm Community gather around the workshop table to start the day with a prayer.
>
> It's a busy time at this 160-hectare, Jesuit-owned farm, which for 24 years has been a home and workplace for a unique community of people with various types of disabilities.
>
> But because of a decline in the number of Jesuit priests, the last residents – volunteer helpers and disabled alike – will be moving out in June.
>
> For now, the measured rhythm of the farm day continues, punctuated by meetings at which community members discuss what has to be done.
>
> Lambs and calves are being born daily. There are chickens to be tended, eggs to be collected, fruit trees to be pruned, branches to be clipped. And someone must be ready to serve customers at the small store that sells eggs, organically raised beef, vegetables in season and handicrafts.

In this community Jesuits and religious Sisters along with lay volunteers had the privilege not just of working with but of sharing life with people who had been pushed to the margins of society. It is often these people, who have the least capacity to fit into our competitive, efficiency-driven society, who excel in gifts that are desperately needed in today's world – gifts such as tenderness and forgiveness, fidelity and loyalty. Some people have said that this community where the distinction between the helpers and the helped is almost obliterated, where, for example, the director of the community shares a room with an ex-prisoner in a relationship of mutual friendship, is folly and even irresponsible and dangerous. Others have described it as one of the most significant experiments in community living in Canada in the twentieth century.

Whatever the truth in these differing viewpoints, what I know is that the 21 years of living here have profoundly shaped and enriched my life. I feel a deep debt of gratitude for the people who have passed through the Farm Community. Some shared horrendous pain and brokenness for which they may have received a measure of comfort and healing. A few may have left just as hurt as when they came. Some lived amazing experiences of transformation and growth. All shared something of themselves and shared in the mystery of human communion as well as communion with the land and the animals.

During the sabbatical time I have taken since the farm closed, I have been able to reflect on and reconnect with soul memories that move me to deep wonder. This reflection urges me to honour the community and celebrate the lives of those who have been a part of it by telling some of its sacred history. I feel a sense of joy as well as obligation in venturing to relate for others the fruit of this reflection.

What I am setting out to do in this book is not to write the history or to give a comprehensive picture of the whole community. I believe that would be a fruitful enterprise, but it lies beyond what I am prepared to do at present. This book is about one member of the Farm Community, Byron Dunn, and my relationship with him during the dozen years that we were together in the community. This was a unique relationship that rooted me in the heart of the community, and it serves to illuminate what this community was all about. I cannot, however, speak about one relationship without speaking about at least a few of the many people who formed the context of that relationship, sustaining and being sustained by it.

Once I began articulating some of the stories of my relationship with Byron I realized that as that relationship was lived within the life of a community, so too the retelling of the story needed to be done in a communal context. So it was that

I spent a week with three former members: Fr. Doug McCarthy SJ, the founder; Fr. Dan Phelan SJ, who joined the community soon after it began and stayed for six years; and Louisa (Weesa) Blair, a community member from 1984 to 1987. Occasionally during this week we were joined by Sr. Liz Budicky, who was in the community from 1985 to 1989, as well as for several months in 2001. It was her community, the Sisters of St. Joseph of Toronto, who so graciously welcomed us into their mother house for this week of storytelling. As well as sharing stories about Byron and many others who had touched our lives, we simply enjoyed being together, experiencing that common understanding and love of life and people that we received from living in this crazy community. I suppose this sense of communion is what veterans of a war experience, having lived something so powerful that no one else could possibly understand and that binds them irrevocably together at some very deep level.

This time together was also a healing process for us as we continue to struggle with the hurt and bewilderment around the closing of the Farm Community. For each of us and, I suppose, for most of those who had been a part of the community, understanding and accepting the closure is a different and very personal affair. I, as the director, had the privilege as well as the pain of being immediately responsible for the relocation of those who were in the community during the final months.

One of the things I knew needed to be done before the actual closing was to give all the former members the opportunity to come back and say their personal goodbyes. I did so by way of a celebration of thanksgiving for all that we had lived here, both the joys and the pains. Thus it was that about 150 people from as far away as St. John's, Newfoundland, and Tacoma, Washington, came together for the weekend of March 25, 2001, to reconnect with one another, to walk the land and visit with the fields and trees and livestock, to laugh, to cry and to pray.

On the Friday evening of this weekend of thanksgiving we held a gathering in one of our homes, the Red House, where people filled the living room, dining room, kitchen and chapel, after having loaded the tables with the food they had brought. We hugged each other with great joy as we met again. There was laughter, there were stories (Byron Dunn figuring in a number of these) and there were tears. The talk had the hush and tenderness that is usually experienced at the wake of a loved one.

The stories, laughter and tears continued the following day. We gathered in the workshop after many had participated in doing the farm chores. Sr. Mary Schneider, then living in the community, led us in prayer, suggesting that we reflect on our time in the community, remembering the joys and the pain. Soon after this we were treated to a pancake lunch with freshly made maple syrup. There were many photo albums available throughout the workshop, the walls were covered with collages of farm and community photos, and an ongoing slide presentation was available. At the end of that cold afternoon, with traces of snow still to be seen along the tree lines and other shaded areas, we came together around a large fire pit by one of the apple orchards. We sang, we prayed and, during a hushed stillness, one by one we offered to the fire a symbolic twig or a piece of paper on which we had written the fruit of our prayer: the things we needed to let go of, the things we needed God's grace to live with. Then, after a sumptuous dinner in Ignatius Hall, a spacious room in the Jesuit Centre there on the farm property, we pushed back the tables and danced and danced. During intermissions taken by the band from the local university community, Paul, a former member of the community, played the fiddle while his wife, Halinka (their wedding had taken place here on the farm), called the square dances familiar to many of us.

On Sunday we were back in this hall to celebrate a final liturgy of communion and thanksgiving. One participant summed it up for me this way: "I went to the mass with a heavy heart, but during your homily the heaviness went away. I am grateful for what I have received. I am not without hope." The mass captured the prayerful and reflective nature of the weekend. We joyfully gave thanks for all that the Farm Community was. We acknowledged that some left the community with much pain, with wounds not healed. We prayed for forgiveness. We prayed for the present members who would be moving to new homes. We acknowledged our own sorrow and prayed that it might give birth to new life. We experienced healing through our communion with each other and through our prayer.

After this liturgy we gathered by the workshop to plant a tree, a beautiful 3-metre-high red oak, first planted as a seedling in the nursery by the Red House. The tree also had a fresh wound on its bark, which had been eaten by hungry rabbits during the past winter. There was also evidence of healed wounds from the past. This tree was a good symbol of the mystery of the community. Each person helped with the planting by placing a handful of soil back in the hole. Then we said our final goodbyes with more laughter and tears, sensing that like this oak tree, something of the community would continue to live on in us and in the thousands who in different ways had been touched by its life.

I am pleased that some former members have directly contributed to the writing of this book by way of quotations I have garnered from several editions of the community newsletters: the earliest version, entitled *The Spreader*, and the later one, *Behind the Barn News*. Also I have incorporated selections from letters Weesa Blair wrote to her parents in England during her stay in the community. These delightful pieces appear at the end of each chapter under the heading "Meanwhile, Back at the Ranch." They don't necessarily relate to the particular chapter; rather, they are like background sketches, giving a feel for what else is happening in the life and work of the farm as the story unfolds. Everyone who shared in the life of the Farm Community up to and including Byron's time there has contributed to this story by helping to shape his and my life and our relationship. Those who came later have contributed by the way they helped to shape my life since that time and my way of understanding and articulating that relationship and its place in the community.

Byron and I lived in the Farm House, one of the community's two homes of welcome. Each of these homes had its own unique culture, which means that the richness of the life and the occupants of the other home, the Red House, will unfortunately be largely missing from this book. More stories need to be told.

I hereby invite the reader to join me in this, my journey with Byron Dunn, an extraordinary man with a remarkable life story, the last dozen years of which I had the privilege to share very intimately. The journey was not always easy, but it was wonderfully challenging and enriching.

I believe that there are extraordinary dimensions of every human person but unfortunately we are not always open or attentive enough to see this. How differently we see through the lens of fear, anger, indifference or love. When we do see something of the goodness or courage or beauty of one person, we are given a glimpse of what is potentially in every person. A fascinating book could be written about pretty well everyone that I have known in the Farm Community. Byron, however, by virtue of the dozen years we shared a room together, has touched me in a very deep way and given me a sense of urgency to tell this story.

There is more about myself in this book than I had originally intended, but it seemed necessary in telling Byron's story to also tell some of my own story and how it shaped and was shaped by my way of relating with this unique man. I hope that what I say about myself will not distract but rather focus the reader's attention on my friend Byron. I hope that you, the reader, will be touched as I have been touched by him and his painful, courageous journey, and that you will, as I did, enjoy a few good laughs along the way. Byron, in spite of and in some ways because of his personal sufferings and struggles, has given me a glimpse into the face of God, and revealed to me something of the beauty and dignity of being human. It is my prayer that he will do the same for you.

1

Don't Sell the Homestead, Mama

It was a clear, crisp autumn day with the maples and other hardwood trees starting to blush into colour, the orchard laden with apples glistening in the morning sun. The cattle corn, standing higher than the tallest man, was dry enough to rustle in the gusting breeze. Wednesday, and a meeting of all of us members of Ignatius Farm Community began just after we had finished the chores of feeding and bedding the animals in our two barns, collecting the eggs and milking our one dairy cow. This was one of our periodic meetings to deepen our understanding of what we were about in our living and working together and how we might do it better or even, at times, how we might survive. The meeting room was in Ignatius College, situated on the Jesuits' 600-acre farm property just north of the city of Guelph, Ontario. It was a building with an increasing amount of unused space since its purpose was for the initial training of men in formation to become Jesuits, and these were diminishing in number. For me this was a place of powerful memories of my own initial formation into religious life.

It was here in this same building, a quarter of a century earlier, in 1956, that I began my training as a Jesuit, the same year that I graduated from the University of Toronto with a degree in Civil Engineering. Every spring on the first weekend of March during my four years of engineering studies I would make a weekend retreat organized by the Newman Club, a group of students on the U of T campus whose aim was to help the Roman Catholic students deepen and enrich their life of faith. I found that this weekend of prayer, which happened to take place at the Jesuit retreat centre, Manresa, in a lovely pastoral setting outside the city, was good nourishment for my relationship with God. More importantly in my consciousness was how it always proved to be an excellent way to get centred and focused for the final month of study for the end-of-term exams in early April. The fact that I never flubbed an exam owed much to this annual spiritual tune-up I received at Manresa.

During the third year that I was doing this retreat, on the Saturday afternoon while browsing in the reading room, I came upon a Jesuit vocation pamphlet. It was probably more the pictures than the words that attracted me: young men in black robes seeming to be very happy together in a classroom, in a chapel and especially in the field playing touch football, a game I dearly loved. The next thing I knew I was doing something I had not done in my two previous retreats: knocking at the door of the priest who was preaching the weekend. As soon as I stepped into his office I found myself saying, "I'm not sure what I'm going to do with my life." Until I spoke it, this had not been a conscious question for me. Even less so the next phrase that came out of me: "Becoming a priest seems ridiculous." When he responded, "What's so ridiculous about it?" I knew at once what I was going to do. He, Fr. Ken Casey SJ, who has since gone to his heavenly reward, invited me to sit down and talk. Since I only had 13 months left to go until graduation, he encouraged me to finish my engineering studies. He also suggested that I look at other options besides the Jesuits, but I left Manresa at the end of the weekend peacefully knowing that after graduation I would join this group of men about whom I knew no more than what was contained in that one-page vocation pamphlet. That Jesuits lived in community seemed to be all I needed to know at that time.

So here I was many years later, in the 1980s, part of this unique community in which only a couple of the members were Jesuits, sitting in a large circle finishing our coffee, tea or juice, waiting for Fr. Doug to begin the meeting. Then a knock came at the door. "I'm sorry to bother you," the intruder began, "but I thought you would want to know that the cattle are in the cornfield."

Before Harry, the farm manager, could say, "Let's go, folks," most of us were already in motion, knowing at least enough about farming to realize that it would not take long for a herd of cattle to do considerable damage tromping around in a cornfield. At the side entrance to the college we put our boots on and headed for the fields. Harry, with long strides, scuffling the gravel with his unlaced boots, was the first to reach the field, even ahead of energetic little Mary D, who ran all the way. Harry, like an army general, quickly assessed the situation and formulated the plan of attack. "There's where they broke through the fence, but we won't try to herd them back through there. We'll spread out on the far side of the field, move them into this lane and then run them up to that far gate."

"Should I saddle up the horses?" asked Mary D, a city girl, who was enjoying every aspect of this new life of farming.

Harry chuckled loudly, but said in a kindly way, "I think we might have them back in their place before you could get a saddle on one of those horses, Mary. Why don't you run to that far corner of the field and start moving them out of the corn. Just wait 'til everyone is in a line and we'll all start into the field together. Tom, you can open the gate and start calling them." Harry knew that, given Tom's size, he would be better on the gate than tramping through the corn behind the cattle. The huge, gentle Tom floated off down the lane towards the gateway.

He was not one for raising his voice so it was good to hear him calling out, "Here coboss, coboss, here coboss!" while the rest of us moved through the cornfield urging the cattle ahead of us: "Hey, hey, come on, come on, move it, move it, heya, heya." This was a very different picture than that of young men in black cassocks playing touch football that had caught my attention many years earlier at the Manresa retreat centre. Nevertheless, the feeling of well-being as I ran through the cornfield with this motley crew of Farm Community members seemed to be a more than adequate fulfilment of the longing enkindled by that vocation pamphlet some 30 years earlier. Having been a pretty good athlete in my younger days, I was now enjoying the physical exertion of the farm work but especially the team effort that it demanded.

Half an hour later we were back in the meeting room, in our stocking feet, exuding the perfumes of sweat, manure and sweet hay, ready for Doug's introduction. Byron, a former truck driver, with no legs for chasing after cattle, had been outside the door enjoying a cigarette when we returned. Had the cattle gotten into a more open field he might have jumped into the truck and run them down that way. He asked how we had managed the roundup, and then mumbled dryly, "Don't sell the homestead, Mama, give the goldarn thing away."

Fr. Doug began the meeting by asking Harry's wife, Peg, to lead us in a prayer. Harry and Peg, along with their five children, had joined the community in the fall of 1979, when someone was needed to manage the farm. They lived in a house just up the highway from the farm. Their sixth and last child, Lizzie, born after they joined the community, was clinging to her mother's knee as Peg prayed that the spirit of truth and love guide us in our sharing and reflections.

We needed that guidance. The community had been founded by Fr. Doug after he had spent some time as a prison chaplain in Guelph. Once their sentences were up, young people were emerging from jail with nowhere to go. Many of them had been rejected by their families and now by society as well. Some were emotionally fragile or mentally ill and bounced back and forth between psychiatric hospitals and prisons, the only places they experienced any security.

What they needed, Doug decided, was unconditional love and acceptance. With the courage and foolishness of a true visionary, he opened a house for ex-prisoners as well as for people with intellectual disabilities who can be especially gifted at accepting others. A few years later, Doug and his people took over the old Jesuit Novitiate farm so that they would have a place to work as well as live. And he invited anyone who was brave or foolish enough to join him in this adventure.

What he attempted to do was about as idealistic and impossible as any venture based on true Gospel values, and as prophetic. He described our way of proceeding as "Four levels, one way." The four levels were unconditional acceptance, intensive caring, non-punishment, the right to love. These four commitments were the one way to live this adventure of community, and they would continue to inspire and challenge the community for the entire 25 years of its existence.

Now Doug was asking the community to take this vision, claim it as our own, and deepen it together.

His inclusion of everyone at this vision meeting was emblematic of the vital belief that the community clung to, and that was both its strength and its weakness. This belief was that everyone has gifts to offer the community, and no one should be excluded from important decisions. The line between volunteers and those welcomed from prison or elsewhere was deliberately blurry. And indeed, people betrayed any categories: often the volunteers demanded more attention or needed as much healing as the others. And, in the minds of some, Doug and I and the other Jesuits were sickest of all, thinking we could make such a community work with so little structure and even with our attempts to hold productive meetings with everyone, and not just those capable of being decision-makers and leaders.

"This community," he began, "has always been full of surprises like the one we just had — cattle interrupting us the minute we start the meeting. We just never know what's going to happen." Doug sat unassumingly in the circle as he spoke with us. He, too, was in stocking feet, having helped with the morning chores and the cattle roundup. "My hope with this community was to create a healing place for people coming from correctional and psychiatric institutions, along with people like you, Bob, whose gifts are more of the heart, gifts of relationship and welcome." Bob, one of the first people welcomed into the community, and the last to leave, beamed lovingly at Doug with his big brown, melancholy eyes. "I also wanted this to be an alternative community for Jesuits and other committed Christians."

When Doug first proposed his idea to the Jesuits in 1976, it was met with some skepticism, most of which was focused on the plan to staff the community with volunteers. For some it was inconceivable that people would come forward to live and work in such a place without pay.

However, after much prayer and discussion, the proposal was approved with strong support on the part of a few and more than a little reticence on the part of those who were convinced that it was too risky and doomed to failure. Thus, on Thanksgiving Day of 1976, the community began. The Red House was opened by Dick and Louise Anstett, along with Doug. Dick and Louise lived in the community for the first four years of its existence, after which they moved into town with their sons, Aaron and Daniel, who were both born in the community. They continued to be close and supportive friends. Many others — lay people, Jesuits and religious Sisters — came for shorter or longer periods, so there was rarely a time when there were not enough people to provide the necessary care and labour.

A year after the opening another Jesuit priest, Dan Phelan, joined the community. Occasionally, younger Jesuits in training came for anywhere from a couple of weeks to a couple of years as part of their formation. It was thought that this experience of living and working in such a mixed community of men, women and children, educated people and very simple people who lived more out of their hearts, would be a good grounding for future priests.

At the time of the community's founding I was living just an hour and a half away in Toronto with the Jesuits of Regis College, the major seminary where the final years of theological training prepared students to be ordained to the priesthood. My primary work was being a spiritual guide for some of these students while at the same time giving spiritual direction and preaching retreats for many others besides the Jesuits.

I had begun this ministry in 1971 upon returning from France where, for a couple of years, I had lived in l'Arche, a community created to welcome people with intellectual disabilities and those willing to share life with them in an atmosphere of faith, trust and mutual relationships. Jean Vanier founded l'Arche in 1964 with the support and inspiration of his spiritual father and friend, the Dominican priest Père Thomas Philippe. The two of them may have begun this community primarily out of compassion for people who seemed to be the poorest of the poor, deeply wounded from birth in their ability to reason and even more deeply wounded by the pain of rejection – sometimes by their own families but constantly by society, which in so many ways tells them and their parents that such people have no place and would have done everyone a favour by not being born. It was not long, however, before Jean and Père Thomas began discovering the incredible gift of these most vulnerable people whose hearts were profoundly open to and capable of relationship with others and with God. Their unique capacity for tenderness, faithfulness and forgiveness seems to make them, more than any others, a revelation of the mystery of God who, according to the Judeo-Christian tradition and most other religions, *is* tenderness, faithfulness and mercy. The communities of l'Arche try to create the conditions of welcome, respect, freedom and prayerfulness that will help people with disabilities to realize their gifts and to offer them to a Church and a world that are in desperate need of such gifts. It was not long before more of these communities were founded: first in Canada by a married couple who were Anglicans, and soon in India where Hindus and Muslims were welcomed. Although it began in the Roman Catholic tradition, it quickly opened to embrace ecumenical and interfaith communities as well. Presently, l'Arche is an international federation of over 120 communities in more than 30 countries.

So while living and working in nearby Toronto, I was keeping an eye on what was happening in Guelph, and was always deeply touched when I visited this new little community that was living out the spirit of l'Arche. Gradually, it became clear to me that I was being called to join my friend Doug in this enterprise. Doug had also been inspired by Jean Vanier and his work. While preparing to be ordained, Doug had sought out Jean for advice about what ministry he should be undertaking as a priest. Jean's advice to Doug was quite simple: "It doesn't matter what you do as long as you build community." Doug spent a summer in France in one of the l'Arche communities there. My own time at l'Arche had deepened my longing for that kind of intentional community focused around people in pain. I still felt that my gifts for spiritual direction and retreats were important, but I sensed that by being rooted in relationships with the people of the Farm Community and grounded in the work of the farm I could claim and use these gifts more effectively. So it was that I came to Guelph in the spring of 1980.

The following year, I was named as the founding director of a Jesuit volunteer program, the Jesuit Companions, a work I was well placed to accomplish from within the Farm Community. This program offered young adults the opportunity to spend a year or so living and working with Jesuits, especially in areas of service with people who were marginalized. The hope of the handful of us Jesuits who designed the program was that it would have a subversive element: these young people would help to transform us and our fellow Jesuits in our way of living community. Many of the companions, beginning with Mary Jo, John and Susan, Weesa, Kevin and Mary D, were assigned to the Farm Community. During the 10 years that I directed this program, 50 or more people took part in it, including several young married couples, some with children. Throughout these years, the Farm Community was the base for the program's summer orientation, so all of the participants had an association with the community, some staying for one or several years at the Farm while others went to Jesuit apostolates around the country. These people brought a great deal of life to the community and to me personally. It seems that for most of them it was an important formation experience in Ignatian spirituality, including the key aspect of the service of faith and justice.

Over the years, the Farm Community welcomed more than 300 people, many of whom had nowhere else to live. Some stayed with us for short periods of time, and some a little longer, such as Larry, who made so much progress in the two years he was here, thanks especially to the support of Harry and Peg and their family, that he was finally able to go back to his own family. Others, such as Bob, Shirley, a woman with severe epilepsy, and Byron made it their permanent home.

As the meeting progressed, Doug spoke of the community and its origins in a way that made everyone feel included – or almost everyone. "It's my home, too, Doug," Mary Makletzoff interjected, with her deep voice that resonated with a subtle mixture of anger and humour.

"That's right, Mary," Doug continued. "You, along with everyone who has come here, no matter for how long, have added their gifts to the community and helped make it what is."

Both the philosophy of Jean Vanier's l'Arche communities and the charism of the Jesuits influenced the spirit of the Farm Community. As a result of this blend of traditions, a unique religious sense developed, one that helped to sustain us in difficult times and created such a powerful and distinct quality and style of life that it held a deep attraction for many people.

It could seem from the outside that this sophisticated and highly educated group of men known as the Jesuits would have little in common with l'Arche or any similar enterprise. The fact is that since my own contact with l'Arche just four years after its founding there have always been Jesuits deeply linked to the l'Arche communities in various parts of the world. St. Ignatius, who founded the Jesuits in 1540 in Rome, was passionately committed to the person of Jesus and knew that the name for the new community had to be *Societatis Jesu*, the Society of Jesus, its members being known as Companions of Jesus. His love for Jesus, who was born in the poverty of Bethlehem and ended his humble earthly journey in the poverty of Calvary, gave him a deep longing to be poor and to be with the poor and rejected. In recent General Congregations the Jesuits have reaffirmed this preferential option for the poor. Ignatius' *Spiritual Exercises,* which shape the inner vision of every Jesuit, are a process of prayer leading to spiritual freedom, a freedom to love and to be attentive and grateful for the way God is loving us at every moment in all things, in all the events of our lives, however glorious or however painful they might be. We are invited to seek and find God even in the most broken people and situations, in beauty and in pain, whether worshipping in a splendid cathedral or shovelling manure in a stinky old barn.

At an international l'Arche gathering held in Rome in 1984, which included directors and pastoral ministers of the various communities from around the world, over a dozen of us Jesuits took part. Fr. Peter Hans Kolvenbach, the General Superior of the Jesuits, spent a few hours with us there. In his brief address to the assembly, he spoke of this close bond between the Jesuits and l'Arche. He said that central to the spirituality of the Jesuits is our prayer "Take, Lord, and receive all my liberty, my memory, understanding, my entire will...give me only Your love and Your grace: that is enough for me." He went on to say that for the people at the heart of l'Arche, this offering has been realized in a very real and complete way, such that they are able to live only by God's love and grace. Thus, he concluded, they are grace to us and we can be grace to them.

So we in the Farm Community saw ourselves as a Christian community rooted in Ignatian spirituality and the spirituality of l'Arche. However, we never excluded people for their beliefs or lack of beliefs. We tried not to make the non-believers feel excluded or like second-class citizens, but we needed to draw nourishment for our lives and our faith by prayer and worship. The Eucharist was very important; it was celebrated weekly as a communal event, and at most important community gatherings. The blessing of the land, New Year's Day mass in the barn, two days of retreat every year, Thanksgiving, Holy Week – all these became an intrinsic part of the community's identity.

For the first three years, the community was limited to the Red House, and people looked for work in town. However, many were not able to find or hold on to employment. This had a demoralizing effect and pointed to the necessity of meaningful work for the process of healing. To meet that need, in 1979 Ignatius College, in response to Doug's request, turned the farm over to our care. The farm had been run for more than 60 years by the Jesuit Brothers, who at this point were few in number and aging. It provided an excellent work base for us. Everyone could find some meaningful work on the farm, in return for a modest stipend, and we took pride in producing most of our own food as well as food for others.

It was at that point that Harry Jonker came with his family to be the farm manager. The Jesuits then purchased the small adjoining farm to the north of the novitiate farm, along with a house that Sr. Christine Leyser opened in 1980, called the Farm House. This would be my home for the next 21 years.

The turning over of the farm to the care of Doug and his ragtag gang was a profound act of faith on the part of those Jesuit Brothers who were and had been running the farm with meticulous care since 1913. The Brothers were men who entered the Jesuits with the intention not to be ordained to the priesthood, but rather to work in service of the priestly ministry of the Order. Their work was mostly manual and they tended to be practical, down-to-earth men of deep and simple faith. The current Brothers watched with no small horror at how we were farming: the way Rick was raking the hay field not by driving the tractor along the wind rows but rather following the seagulls that he was sure were giving him directions, or the way gates would be left open, allowing the cattle to roam through the vegetable gardens or graze on the retreat centre lawn, or the way Fred would sit in the middle of the henhouse allowing the chickens to roost on his head and shoulders and lay eggs in his lap, or the way the equipment would be mistreated so that hours of time had to be spent on easily avoidable repairs. The Brothers would shake their heads and pray for the survival of the farm and its keepers. Brother Dan would say in wonderment, "The Jesuits have spent thousands of dollars educating these priests, and there's McCarthy and Clarke down

there in the barn forking manure – it just doesn't make sense."
They were, however, men of faith who somehow trusted Doug
and me, and we in turn found great support in their friendship
with us and with our people. In their love for the person and
life of Jesus and their vocation to serve him with the work of
their hands, they were able to intuit that some fundamental
Christian truth and Ignatian vision were being lived out in this
messy little community.

When Brother Hugo came back from Africa, we asked him
to come and work on the farm repairing machinery. He was
dubious about the idea but the provincial superior told him to
come and see. After a week he came to Doug and said he
couldn't possibly stay, there was too much chaos and no one
seemed to be in charge. So Doug gave him a copy of the Four
Levels and told him to read it. Hugo took one level every
morning and prayed on it. At the end of the week he said,
"Now I can see what you are up to. Nothing we did in Africa
was as hard as what you are trying to do here." Hugo, a holy
man, was able to make that switch in understanding. He stayed
and was an immense help because he had worked in Africa and
could make do with whatever he had. In Africa you couldn't
just go off to the dealership to get a new part. You had to make
one. All he could see was chaos when he started in our workshop,
but he put order into it that we never had before or since.

Meanwhile, I was discovering, along with Doug and with
the inspiration of the Brothers, that forking manure and all the
other things that running a farm entailed, and doing this in
communion with people who for various reasons had been
marginalized from society, was exactly where I wanted to be
and where, as a Jesuit priest, I was feeling called to be, in spite
of my many years of urban living and my training in engineering,
philosophy and theology.

Having summarized the history and spirit, Doug invited us
to reflect upon these questions: What do I like about the

community? What does the community mean to me? What is my image of the community?

The sharing around these questions was varied and animated. There were the simple clear statements, such as Bob's: "I like the people, I have friends here," and Mary Makletzoff's: "I like feeding the chickens and collecting the eggs." Michael Allen, revealing his intensely religious attitude, said, "I have lots of love and respect for each person and for the animals – God is so present in everything we do here. I wish everyone could get to experience this." Someone else said, "The image I have of the community is that of a garden: every member is a seed that grows differently according to our different backgrounds, some higher and faster, others stay small, some are close to the ground like pumpkins while others reach up like the pine trees." John said the community was "a place where I can answer the three important questions in life: can I love well, can I learn to let go, and can I live fully each day?" I spoke of the community as being a home for the heart, a place where we can be rooted and where we help each other know and love ourselves.

When Joe Guitar talked about how he liked caring for the animals, Michael suddenly exploded. "You say you like caring for the animals, but I've seen you hitting the cows when you think nobody's looking. You don't care for the cows at all. You hate the cows. I don't know why Harry lets you get away with how you treat the animals."

Joe, a little guy, also with a fiery temper, jumped to his feet and with clenched fists started towards Michael. "I don't have to take that bullshit from you, you don't know what the hell you're talking about."

Michael was on his feet, shouting back, "You don't belong here, you should be, you should be back in jail where you belong, you should…."

Harry jumped between them, saying, "Okay, you guys, cool it, that's enough."

Michael continued, "I don't have to cool anything, I know what I'm talking about. He's the one that needs to cool it, and stop beating the cows." Then he stormed out of the room. Harry started to follow Michael but Doug said, "It's all right, Harry. I'll go talk with him." Joe resumed his seat with an irritating smirk on his face, while an awkward silence hung in the room.

I was always unnerved by Michael's angry outbursts. I was aware, however, of his gentler side. He had a special love for the cattle and was amazingly gifted at dealing with them. Trying to herd the cattle from one field to another, or trying to get a newborn calf to nurse from its mother, Michael would speak gently and reverently with the animals and they seemed to understand and want to please him. So I was becoming a little less frightened of his anger, especially as I befriended him and came to appreciate how courageously he struggled with what he himself could name as paranoid schizophrenia. While I always found these conflicts disturbing, Byron, on the other hand, sat calmly through this and other such fights without the slightest upset. With the family life he had known in rural New Brunswick, fights probably made him feel more at home.

Doug returned a few minutes later and announced, "Michael feels better going back to work right now, but he will join us for lunch." Then the sharing continued.

These reflection meetings were significant moments, refocusing us on the essentials, helping us appreciate one another and value what we were receiving as we lived and worked together and helping the more recent arrivals to understand what this unique community was all about.

What remained in me from this particular meeting was first my deep sense of satisfaction about what I was now doing with my life. I had my struggles and fears, but at least at this moment I was content and felt certain I was in the right place. Second, it was Byron's painfully blunt statement that came at the end of all the sharing. Doug finally turned to him and asked, "So what does the community mean to you, Byron?" Without a moment's hesitation he responded in his muffled, raspy voice, "If I wasn't here, I'd be dead." Clearly none of us understood better than he the meaning and importance of the Farm Community.

★ ★ ★ ★ ★

MEANWHILE, BACK AT THE RANCH

Dear Mum and Dad,

Sometimes I have to wonder if God isn't just laughing his head off at us. We have been cleaning out the two cattle pens over in this barn. We let the cows out into the barnyard, and drive in and out with a front-end loader bringing out the manure and tipping it over the barnyard gate into either of two manure spreaders, driven by Mary D and me. When the spreader is full we drive it down the farm lane along the swamp and dump it two fields away on a long manure heap to compost. So when it works efficiently it all goes very smoothly.

Well first of all Mary D got her load and drove off to the heap, while I was starting the other tractor around the corner. I came down the hill towards the barnyard and all the cattle were streaming up the hill towards me. Mary D had got the spreader caught on the gate as she drove through, and had driven off dragging the gate behind her without noticing. The cattle were prancing joyfully out into the fields that were two feet deep in snow. We mustered up four people and positioned the tractors to try and herd them back, which took about an hour as they had found the silage pad, heaven on earth, and didn't want to leave it. Meanwhile Jezebel was dancing around trying to catch snowflakes as they fell.

Jezebel is the farm's Australian Blue Heeler, supposedly a dog bred for herding cattle. They are taught to herd them by nipping at their heels. But the only heels Jezebel ever nipped are the heels of the nuns and priests who are making a retreat at Loyola House and walk solemnly around the farm deep in contemplation. So she was banished to our end of the farm.

Finally we got the cattle back and I suddenly saw that the other gate was open, as our original intention had been to herd them back through that gate. So they were just about to stream out the other side of the barnyard. I flung myself through the snowdrifts and over the fence and just managed to close the gates in time. Then, feeling exhausted but proud, I got back on my tractor and tried to move it from the clever position someone had parked it in to blockade the cattle. I couldn't back it up, I could only go forward, and Kevin confidently signalled me to drive across the lawn, where my wheels sank deep into a snowdrift. Two more people tried to get it out but it simply got firmly lodged up against a nice new wire fence. We had to get a tractor, a chain and a cable to pull out the spreader and the tractor one by one, and we pretty well wrecked the fence. But at least we were set to go again. By then it was lunch time. After lunch I took my first load out, and the apron chain (it moves all the manure from the front to the back of the spreader) busted. I had to tie it up with hay string to make it to the pile, fork off the whole load by hand, which took a good hour and a half, and then drive to the shop to repair the chain. Meanwhile Mary D took another load out, and on the way back the snow chains on one of the tires broke and wrapped itself securely around the axle, and she had to walk home.

Can you imagine such a day? We might as well have spent the day as Jezebel did, leaping up in the air snapping at snowflakes.

Bill says every morning I should spend a few seconds thanking God for the gift of today. This morning I woke up and said, "Thank you, God, for the gift of today. Please don't let it be like the gift of yesterday."

Lots of love,

Weesa

2

Lord, You Have Seduced Me

It was April 15, 1980, a cool, cloudy evening. I had visited the Farm House once before, but now that I was arriving to live here it was as if I was seeing it for the first time. It was a storey-and-a-half red brick house built in the late 1800s, and little effort had been made to hide its age. No walkway or path approached the front door, which looked mournfully on to a rough and poorly kept front lawn bordering a busy two-lane highway, beyond which a subdivision of upper-middle-class homes was under construction. A gravel driveway running past a side door continued on another 50 feet to the barn. Covering this side door was an open porch that stretched along half the length of the house. Entering the house through this door, I found myself in the spacious kitchen, which apparently also served as the dining room. The large dining table was covered by a faded red-and-white-checkered oilcloth, and was surrounded by about 10 wooden chairs, none of which matched either the table or each other. Beside the door was a range of coat hooks loaded down with an assortment of coats, coveralls and caps, the smell of which clearly indicated they had spent an awful lot of time in the barn. In the corner was a large woodbox piled high with logs. Some of them, it seemed, would be a challenge for even me to lift, and I prided myself on my strength, which in my mind more than adequately compensated for my short stature. In my younger days I had eagerly participated in such rugged sports as football and boxing.

Set out from the middle of the back wall was a black cast iron wood-burning stove, standing firmly on short, angular legs, and smiling with two big eyes (the draft wheels in its front doors). It gave a warm, friendly presence to the whole room, not to mention sending out waves of heat to ward off the chill of this spring evening. I immediately felt an affinity to this dominant figure, sensing that we were destined to become good friends. Through a windowed door leading to the back porch I could see a strip of lawn dominated by a magnificent black walnut tree. A page wire fence separated the lawn from a low-lying pasture that phased into a marsh of bulrushes with a backdrop of cedars interspersed with poplar trees.

Covering the kitchen floor were large mottled green and cream squares of industrial tiles. The beige paint of the wainscotting around the walls was scratched and flaked off in places, revealing the previous coating of dark brown. The rest of the walls and ceiling were off-white, darkened by the smoke of the wood stove and, as I would later learn, from many a cigarette. I felt unnerved by the rundown feel of the place, which was so strikingly different from the orderly religious institutions I had become accustomed to over the past quarter of a century. My nervousness was slightly tempered by a reminiscence of my childhood home in the country, but I felt as if I were heading into that scary, swampy area near that home where my mom always warned me not to go.

Sr. Christine, a small, wiry, energetic woman around my own age, late 40s, welcomed me eagerly. She asked if I would like a cup of tea or anything, but before I got around to responding she was leading me through into the living room. As we entered it, she pointed to a narrow room off to the right:

"That's the chapel, our prayer room," she informed me, but did not give me time to see it. I was already having trouble keeping up with this dynamo of a woman, who was later to be nicknamed the Flying Nun. The living room, which was much cooler than the kitchen due to its distance from the wood stove, was even more unnerving.

The TV set at the far end of the room was blaring with some kind of cop show. It was being watched with varying levels of interest by the four young men in the room. They were seated on a hodgepodge of worn and unmatched chesterfields and armchairs, some of them sloppily covered with colourful but tasteless afghans trailing onto the orangey-red shag carpet. "Here he is, Bill Clarke, the man we've all been waiting for," Christine announced playfully. Then she introduced them to me. "This is Larry." Larry a husky, curly-haired guy in his late teens seemed to be the youngest of the group. He reluctantly turned away from the cop show just long enough to grunt "Hi" without really looking at me. Dougie and Aidan were both more responsive, getting up to shake my hand and say:

"Hi, welcome to the Farm House."

"Hello, welcome. I hope you're going to like it here."

Then Christine, turning to the man sitting in the corner, a slight-built but tough, intense-looking fellow in his mid-20s, said, "This is Gordie." I was pretty sure Gordie heard her, but he made no response. He was somewhere off in another world, probably reliving his own cop show. Christine told me that David, a Jesuit novice, with us for a few more weeks, would be in a little later, and that the other member of the household, Barry, was out and she hoped he would be home later but she could never be quite sure with him. I gazed past her at the pale green walls and the flimsy beige drapes on the windows. I was a long way from home, getting deeper into the swamp.

At the far end of the room to the right of the TV, a doorway opened onto the tiny front hall, from which a staircase led up to the second floor. Straight ahead was a door, which Christine opened, saying, "This is your room, but first let me show you the upstairs." I followed her up the creaky stairs into a hallway that led to four bedrooms and a small bathroom at the far end. She pointed out that there were two men sharing each of the bedrooms, one of which was not much bigger than a closet and had bunk beds. Christine occupied the fourth bedroom, which was next to the bathroom, an even smaller closet-sized room with a bunk bed which she said she shared with women guests. She would eventually share it with Mary Makletzoff, who was welcomed two years later. I heaved a sigh of relief that I was going to be in the room downstairs, presuming it had to be better than anything up here.

So back down we went and I followed Christine into "my" room. It was just wide enough for twin beds with a small table between them, on the right side of which were a stack of pill bottles, a full ashtray, some soggy napkins and a jack-knife. A single wooden chair in the room was draped with clothes. "Your roommate, Byron, is not here right now."

Trying not to show my dismay, I said, "Oh, that's nice." But to myself I was saying, "My roommate? You mean there will be two of us living in this tiny room? What on earth have I gotten myself into?" I was now hopelessly lost and sinking deeper into the swamp. I tried to console myself by noting that the room did have two windows, one on each of the exterior walls, and to the right, at the foot of my roommate's bed, was a door leading into the prayer room. The wallpaper looked as if it had once been a pattern of silver leaves on an ivory background, but over the years the silver and ivory had ceased to do battle and settled for a kind of truce of creamy, dirty grey. A worn green carpet covered most of the floor. Along the wall at the foot of my bed were two small dressers squeezed together, one of them behind the door I was still clinging to. I stepped into the room and closed the door behind me, hoping to block out the sound of the TV but, alas, I could still hear all too clearly the police sirens, the screeching of tires, the crashing of vehicles, accompanied by Larry's enthusiastic "Wow, look out, gettum." I was now up to my neck and still sinking.

I thought with longing of the spacious room and office in the large residence I was leaving behind in Toronto, where I had been living and working as a spiritual mentor for Jesuit students, young men preparing to be ordained as priests. It was not always the most tranquil existence, but suddenly it seemed to me a place of wondrous order, peace and, most of all, privacy. This was a radically different kind of community than anything I had lived with my fellow Jesuits, where all I had to do to indicate I didn't want to be disturbed was to tie a white handkerchief on the knob of my closed door.

Christine explained that Byron, who had arrived a month earlier from the correctional centre, was presently in the Toronto General Hospital for yet another surgery for the ongoing reconstruction of his badly disfigured face. And as if that wasn't enough to make me uneasy, I learned that his two years in prison were for attempted murder. I was going under and could almost smell and taste the slimy swamp water.

It only occurred to me much later that Byron's arrival in the Farm House would have been equally traumatic. He was leaving behind the sterile, impersonal and highly controlled prison environment to share a room "with a priest, for God's sake."

This was the hallowed space where our very different life journeys would intersect and become inextricably linked.

As I stood there with my back pressed against the door, trying to absorb what Christine was saying about my roommate and my new home, I reminded myself that I had chosen to come here, believing that this was a call from God. As a Jesuit how many hundreds of times had I not prayed: "Take, Lord, receive all my liberty, my memory, my understanding, and my entire will, all that I have and possess. Thou hast given all to me. To Thee, O Lord, I return it. All is Thine, dispose of it wholly according to Thy will. Give me Thy love and Thy grace, for this is sufficient for me." But right then it was not this prayer but rather a line from the prophet Jeremiah that was speaking to me: "Lord, you have seduced me and I let myself be seduced." Maybe I was here for God's sake, but would I survive? It was going to take far more than a white handkerchief to protect me from the blaring TV and from the man with the disfigured face convicted for attempted murder who would be sleeping just an arm's-length away in that next bed.

Just then I heard a voice saying, "Bill, Bill, are you all right?" As Christine came back into focus I said to her, "I'll take that cup of tea now."

★ ★ ★ ★ ★

MEANWHILE, BACK AT THE RANCH

Dear Mum and Dad,

This morning I went out and fed and bedded the cows and pigs, trying to avoid the flying heels of the calves. I sympathized with a cow in labour who was wandering around with her back arched and her sides heaving. Then this afternoon I went and bought myself a new pair of workboots. I'm fed up with wearing rubber boots, which are always full of hay, straw, silage, poo, etc.

The calf was born just a couple of hours ago. The slightly older ones are already playing games with each other. Yesterday we herded the cattle right across the farm on horseback. Harry says before you start, you have to explain to them exactly what you want them to do, very carefully. Turn left through this gate, then down the lane, through that gate and across McGladery's, across the middle of the Wet Field, right at Jim Deshaye's rocks (he wired up some boulders and hung them on a fencepost to stop it from falling over), across the stream, left, and through the gate *not* into the cedar bush but straight onwards to the Farm House Barn... It helped me a lot to explain all this to the cows because I realized what I was planning to do with them myself.

Patches the horse knew just what to do. She's a wonderful old horse, she worked so hard without even thinking about it until we were finished, when she stopped and hung her head and the sweat just poured off her. You have to really shout and bellow at the cows, but the horse knew I wasn't shouting at her. By the end I was hoarse and she was horse.

We have two new people here which is a bit of a shock. One is a guy who has been in all sorts of businesses and all sorts of marriages and none of them have worked. He's huge and tall and loves cooking and cleaning and sewing, knitting and ironing. I think his main problem is that he should have been a woman. He is very gentle and cries easily. Then the other is an ultra-heavy-duty guy in his late 20s who has also been in all kinds of businesses and made tons of money, mostly I suspect in quite shady ways. He wears chains around his neck and a huge gold ring with diamonds in it, leather jacket, etc. He is deeply in trouble with the law and hopelessly in debt. He went off to the local mental hospital for an assessment, telling everyone he had "gone to settle his business affairs." He is delightful, with a fantastic sense of humour, and has thrown himself into life here with incredible generosity. I think the place is touching his heart.

Lots of love,
Weesa

3

I'll Live Where Thousands Wouldn't

Once I got settled into the Farm House, I went several times to visit Byron in the hospital, where he was recovering from a 13-hour operation. He hoped it was the last of a series of operations to undo some of the damage caused by an accident that had destroyed everything from his jaw to just beneath his eyes. The details of this terrible event I was to hear from Byron much later. The surgery had involved taking bone from his hip and skin from his chest and stomach in order to construct a new jaw and a pair of feelingless lips. Since nothing could be done to rebuild his nose, he would have to make do with a plastic one fashioned for him and attached to a pair of heavy-rimmed glasses.

On my first visit, Byron was propped up in bed with his face bandaged from just below his eyes and with intravenous tubes running into his arm and oxygen being pumped through a hole in his neck, which I was soon to learn was a tracheotomy. He was expecting my visit, as Christine had been in the day before and told him I was coming. Approaching his bed I grasped the outstretched hand he offered to me and returned the gaze from his sunken, cloudy, grey blue eyes. We held on to this hand and eye communication for some time, as though one of

47

us was clinging to the other who had just slipped off the edge of a precipice. It wasn't clear which one was being rescued. Feeling the strength and the need in his firm but trembling grip helped me overcome my initial insecurity. "It is good to meet you," I said. "How are you doing?" He took a slate and wrote "Thanks for coming." Only then did I turn to the middle-aged man sitting quietly at the foot of the bed and introduce myself. He told me his name was Bob, an old truck-driving buddy of Byron's. When I told him I was from Guelph, he presumed that I also had done time in the prison there, which drew a painful chuckle out of Byron. I was grateful for Bob's presence since conversation with Byron was going to be awkward. Between the three of us we managed a laboured discussion about the weather, the price of gas and the length of time Byron expected to be in the hospital.

The next time I visited, Byron was looking poorly. In response to my greeting he scrawled on his slate "infection." When the nurse came in to check his IV she explained that they were pumping him with antibiotics to try to combat an infection that threatened to undo what was otherwise a successful surgery and to put the restoration work back to the beginning. She went on to say, only half jokingly, "We're doing everything in our power to get 'Tiger' here well and on his way so he doesn't have to come back again." She looked at Byron with a wary smile, saying, "Now, don't you dare try getting up again without calling for assistance." I'm not sure if his effort at a wink was for the nurse or for me but, in any case, it was clear that Byron was no small challenge to the patience of the staff. When we were alone again, he wrote, "I hate hospitals." Then, in response to my comment on how awful it would be to have the surgery fail and have to be repeated, seemingly without fear or self-pity and with a bit of glint in his eye, he wrote "I'll live where thousands wouldn't." I found myself warming to this man whose toughness freed him from any submissiveness to the staff and who seemed far from being overwhelmed by the dreadfulness of his situation.

The infection eventually cleared up. On my final visit all the bandages were gone and Byron was able to speak, although very indistinctly in a deep, raspy voice. I had to ask him to repeat several times before I understood that he was saying "I'm glad to see you." Conversation was a struggle but it was not difficult for us just to be together. We watched a period of NHL hockey on his small TV set, at the end of which, as one more beer commercial began, he said, or at least I think he said, "That's enough of that bullshit" and turned it off. I could see that he was getting tired and it was time for me to go but I was already so comfortable with him that I felt no relief that our visit was over. As we shook hands and said goodbye, there was a look of genuine gratitude in his eyes and a feeling of trust in his firm grip. He was no longer an ex-convict to be feared but rather a fellow traveller on the same road. I found myself thinking as I left the hospital that if I had to share a room with someone, then maybe this guy was not such a bad choice.

When Byron returned to the Farm House he came back into *his* room, where he had spent a month before my arrival. I welcomed him with mixed feelings, since the room was henceforth no longer *mine* but *ours*. In preparation for this moment I had constructed a second, flimsy wardrobe so that we each had a place to hang our clothes, and on the previous evening I had done my best to clean up my side of the room. The most important preparation, however, was begging God to help me make a place in my life and in my heart for this roommate of mine.

Since he had stayed alone in the room for several weeks before going off to the hospital, he was able to move back in as though it was as much his room as it was mine, which indeed it was. He had left a sweater and a couple of shirts in one of the dressers, so no discussion was needed about which was mine or his. The wardrobe I had built fitted into the corner nearest the foot of his bed so it was obvious that it should be for his use, and he liked the fact that it had no door to fuss with. My plan to eventually put a door or at least a curtain on it never materialized. On my side of the small table between our beds, I had a travel alarm clock and a book or two. In the middle was a lamp we could both use, and the rest of the surface was taken up by Byron's numerous medications, shaving kit, carton of cigarettes, ashtray, coffee cup, glasses with the plastic nose attached, and eventually a large cup to store the false teeth he got several years later. The chair in front of the table was used only as a shelf and clothes rack. I hung my things on my side and Byron did the same on his. It was usually Byron's stuff on the seat: Kleenex box, magazines, coffee cups, ashtray, and so forth. Over our two dressers I had installed a shelf for my books. This entire disposition of the space seemed to just happen without discussion. Byron was so exhausted for the first few days that he slept much of the time, thus reducing conversation to a bare minimum. Neither one of us had an excess of material possessions, so the sharing of storage area was not going to be a source of tension.

By the time Christine picked him up the day he was released from prison, Byron's life had been pared down to the bare necessities. On the way to the Farm House they stopped at a store where he sent Christine in to buy him a watch and a jackknife, Byron being afraid to show himself in public. This was a fear that was to remain with him for many months. Other than his few clothes, the watch and knife were his only possessions when he arrived. I still have this knife with its solid black bone handle that fits nicely into the palm of the hand and two foldout blades, one narrower and more sharply pointed.

My life had gone through some paring down as well, but nothing compared to his. I was born into a poor family, the last of four children during the worst years of the Great Depression. I considered myself fortunate to get hand-me-down clothing from my older siblings. My brother Rob, the eldest, was two when our sister Betty arrived. A year later Gord came along and finally, two years later, I was born. My mother, born in Toronto, with some African heritage from both her parents, received her Roman Catholic faith from her Irish maternal grandmother. She worked at various housekeeping jobs until she married. My Jamaican-born father, who immigrated to Canada at the age of 20, had been raised as an Anglican, although his maternal grandmother was of Jewish origin. Dad had to scrape and scrounge to provide for us. In later years, as I listened to my parents reminisce about those days, I got the sense that as hard as things were they were not unhappy times. Most of their stories seemed to have a humorous or happy twist to them. Since Dad had no permanent job in those early days he had to take any little part-time thing he could get – cleaning out someone's basement, washing windows and so on. One of the ways he managed to help put a little bread on the table was to buy several varieties of cheap coffee, mix them together and sell them as an expensive blend. This was a tiny little enterprise that had to involve door-to-door marketing, all of which was probably quite humiliating. Nevertheless, their later description of this made it sound like the greatest of fun. Then there was the time just before Christmas when they were desperately out of money and at their wits' end. Mom happened to open the Bible and discovered a $10 bill she had hidden there many months earlier and then forgotten. Her joyful exclamation still rang with excitement many years later: "Oh, there is a Santa Claus, there is a Santa Claus!"

In 1936, when I was four years old, on my mother's initiative we rented for the summer a tiny ramshackle house on the outskirts of Oakville, an hour bus ride from Toronto. At the time this was a town of about 4,000 inhabitants with only a handful of black families. Mom found that it was getting oppressive to be living in downtown Toronto sharing the home of her aunt and uncle. As the summer came to an end she convinced Dad to buy the house and stay there. The owners only very reluctantly accepted to sell, since they could not bear the thought of a family of six living in such shabby and cramped conditions. The little, whitewashed stucco house had only a kitchen, a living room and two tiny bedrooms that were even smaller than Sr. Christine's in the Farm House. A small bed and dresser left very little floor space in the bedrooms. We three boys shared one of these rooms with bunk beds, where I was always the one to double up with either Rob or, more commonly, Gord. I preferred the top bunk. When Dad was on the road, since by then he had permanent work with the CNR Railway and could be gone for 10 days or more when he was running to Vancouver, Betty shared with Mom the other room, which was also fitted with bunk beds. When Dad was home he and Mom slept in the living room on a pull-out chesterfield. There was a sink in the kitchen with running water, but the house had no indoor toilet. We bathed in a galvanized tub that would be placed in the middle of the kitchen and filled with water heated on the coal-burning stove, which we used for both heating and cooking. It was while standing in that tub at the age of five while Mom was bathing me that I asked for her hand in marriage. Her amused but graceful refusal saddened my little heart but I continued to love her, a love that deepened and matured over the years.

I thoroughly enjoyed the dozen years that we lived there before returning to Toronto. During that time some improvements were made to the house, namely patching and covering the rickety floors, partitioning the kitchen to create a bathroom and eventually adding a long, narrow room that we called the sunroom. This was a family room during the day but my sleeping room at night, which I loved even though it was very cool in the winter since the heat from the kitchen stove did not readily flow into it.

The $400 cost of the house and good-sized lot Dad was gradually able to pay off, mainly from the tips he earned as a porter, one of the few jobs available to blacks until after the Second World War. Within the black community this was considered a respectable career. However, along with his fellow porters Dad found the disrespect, insults and abuse they were constantly subjected to almost unbearable. To keep their jobs they simply had to take it all with a smile. They maintained their dignity and gradually managed to fight for their rights, but this they had to do with the utmost discretion and diplomacy. So from my parents I learned not to strike back but to turn the other cheek, to be a peacemaker. Certainly my passive personality and my need to please others were all part of this mix. Most of the racial slurs I received in my early school days I did my best to ignore, although some of them did cut deeply even through my thick, protective shell. When one older big guy insisted in the presence of my peers on calling me a nigger over and over again and laughingly warded off my feeble efforts to punch and kick him, I felt helplessly humiliated – even more so when he maintained that as a matter of fact that was simply what I was. I realized he was just too ignorant to know this was a pejorative term, but that did nothing to lessen the pain. Once I sent in an application to join the Cub Scouts; a year and a half later the woman in charge stopped me on the street to ask if I was still interested in joining. In a little town like Oakville there was certainly no waiting list. It gave me a feeling of freedom and maturity to be able to look her in the eye and say, "Thanks, I'm no longer interested." Excelling in sports was my way of getting beyond the burden of discrimination. Playing baseball, football and hockey gave me a strong sense of my own worth and created some wonderful friendships.

The weapon Dad encouraged us to take into battle was education. He did not want any of his children to be forced as he was to do such humiliating work. I still remember that when I had to fill out any forms for school that asked for father's profession, he would insist that I put it down as *sleeping and dining car attendant* and not as *porter*. This very word was a symbol for him of humiliation and servitude. He was immensely proud when I graduated with a degree in Civil Engineering, the first university graduate in the family.

From both my parents, but especially from my mother, I received the gift of faith. This was a faith in God and not so much in the Church, although Sunday mass was always an important family event. Even Dad, who was of the Anglican tradition, would sometimes accompany us across town to St. Andrew's, in those days the only Catholic Church in Oakville. Since none of us children were enrolled in the one-room school associated with the parish, we participated, however reluctantly, in Fr. Harris' Sunday afternoon catechism classes. This was the extent of our involvement in parish life. My mother had made one attempt to join the Catholic Women's League but did not feel welcomed. The warmth and kindness that Fr. Harris always showed to our family and to me personally kept me close to the Church. That closeness continued as we returned to Toronto and I continued my studies through high school and university.

When after my graduation I announced that in three months I would be entering the Jesuits to begin training as a priest, Mom was surprised and delighted, while Dad was shocked and dismayed. From that time on he would speak to every priest and nun he met on his train run between Toronto and Montreal. Over the years he came to realize that my change in career was neither a waste of my education nor a loss of respectability. I remember how proud he was in 1953 when my sister's picture appeared in the *Toronto Daily Star* with an article announcing the fact that she, "the first Negro to enter St Joseph's Hospital Nursing School," was graduating with top honours. So I know that if he had lived long enough he would have been equally proud to see my photo in the June 6, 1966, edition of the same daily newspaper with the accompanying article:

> A former high school football star and intercollegiate boxer became the first Canadian-born Negro to be ordained as a priest Saturday.
>
> Rev. William T. Clarke, 33, was ordained in the Jesuit order of the Roman Catholic Church ...
>
> The Toronto-born son of a Jamaican immigrant, Father Clarke will celebrate his first high mass Sunday in St. Brigid's Church.

My commitment to a life of poverty, chastity and obedience, along with my family upbringing, helped to ease my way into life in the Farm House and sharing a room with Byron. What I was not prepared for and what loomed as a huge challenge was the loss of personal space. Byron at least had his two years in prison as training in how to live with little or no privacy. This felt to me like a poverty beyond anything I had known in my childhood and certainly beyond anything for which my Jesuit life had prepared me in spite of my vow of poverty. How would I be able to live it, and live it with a grateful heart? I was being invited to walk on water, and my only hope lay in the certitude that this was humanly impossible.

It is true that in my growing-up years I had shared a room and in the earliest years even a bed with my brother Gord, and lived in a doll-size home with five others, but then I was a child and that was family, that was where I was loved and accepted, that was where I belonged. At the outset I believed that the Farm House was where I belonged because I had felt called by the Spirit and had been assigned there by my Jesuit superior. It would take some time before I acquired an inner sense of belonging, and before I would experience my housemates as family and my roommate as a brother.

Over the months and years and in bits and pieces I learned Byron's story. A year older than me, he had grown up by the Miramichi River in New Brunswick with two older and two younger brothers. His dad was a hard, tough heavy drinker who never backed away from a fight. Byron delighted in recounting how his dad, a horse trader, would use all the tricks of the trade, such as putting bootblack on the face of a horse he was selling to disguise the grey hairs, hoping it wouldn't rain and streak the bootblack down the horse's face. Byron took after his dad, except that he preferred trucking to trading. He was a heavy smoker and drinker by the time he reached his teens. He was only average height and weight but he fought with all comers, no matter how big they might be. When he was drinking, which was often, there was no telling what he might do, to the point where his own brothers were afraid of him. He once told me that he even took on his dad a few times but always got badly beaten, since his dad never hesitated to whack him with a two-by-four or anything else he could get his hands on. It was his dad, Byron told me, who instructed him to "hit first and ask questions later." His mother, in his eyes, was a woman of great faith and patience. Stories about his growing-up years were usually shared at times when we were playing cards or in those quiet moments when we just sat together after having our fill of cards. The drinking, the fighting, even with his dad, he would talk about as a matter of fact, with neither any manifest pride or shame, the simple recounting of an accepted way of life. I listened with rapt attention to life stories that were dramatically different from my own.

In any case, as different as our stories may have been, here we were, the two of us in this little room. That first night, Byron was already in bed with the light out when I came into the room, which smelled of stale cigarette butts. As I slipped off my shirt and pants and hung them on my chair post I was happy that it was dark and that, judging from his laboured breathing, he was asleep. Rolling into bed I was surprised to hear his muffled "Good night, Pal." As I responded, "Good night, Byron, sleep well," I was equally surprised at my own feelings: an odd mixture of strangeness tinged with a certain familiarity — like maybe I'd been here before.

★ ★ ★ ★ ★

MEANWHILE, BACK AT THE RANCH

Dear Mum and Dad,

Life has been going quite quickly and is difficult. I have been turfed out of my room so I don't get poisoned by urea formaldehyde, and all the community vehicles have broken down so we are getting supplies by foot. Byron is drinking again, and then last night Shirley beat up Barbara at the Red House. Bill is away, and it's not full moon, but there's something unsteady in the air.

I got a proposal of marriage yesterday from a middle-aged farmer who lives up the road. He has 100 beautiful acres overlooking Guelph Lake and a lovely old stone farmhouse. It was an experience to be courted by him. We were buying straw from him and I spent most of the day there in between loads. He watched me throwing bales as if I were a work horse in the ring, and obviously approved of my physical strength. He took me into his house and gave me apples and homemade wine, talking beautifully and non-stop to me like a poem as we stood around on the newspaper on the kitchen floor (so he doesn't have to take his boots off), and later on he showed me piles of antique furniture in the barn, promising me it will all be mine if I would take his hand.

In the afternoon the men insisted that I take Tom with me as protection. Tom is 6'3" and weighs at least 250 lbs. After working together for a while, the farmer says,

"You're trying to frighten me, aren't you. I can see there's a high price for you, my dear."

"You're darn right," I said. He laughed ruefully and a bit angrily.

Of course the community is dead set on me marrying him, especially Doug McCarthy, as it would be a lovely property to add to the place, the only price to pay being one human life.

Love,

Weesa

4

I Don't Want Out, I Want Help

There was a deep wound in Byron that never healed and at times would fester into what seemed to be unbearable pain. As trust between us grew he was able to share with me more of his tragic journey, awful memories that as much as possible he tried to keep out of his consciousness. When he did speak about them it was usually in the privacy of our room as we sat on our beds facing one another. The stories came out almost like confessions, usually in times of depression when he could no longer keep them suppressed. At first, only Fr. Doug, Christine and I were privy to this painful history, but gradually he was able to share it with a few others in the community as well.

The woman Byron married in New Brunswick, with whom he had three daughters, must have been quite remarkable to cope as well as she did with this wild husband of hers. They moved to Ontario in the mid-50s where Byron almost always worked as a trucker. Even during his stint in the army he drove trucks most of the time. His few years in the army, Byron said, helped him gain a modicum of decency, order and cleanliness that he had never learned growing up.

For a brief period he had a job driving a local bus route at a time when his drinking was more out of control than usual.

He was in no way remorseful as he spoke of how he would pull over to the curb and announce to the passengers that there was some problem with the engine. Then, going around to the rear of the bus, he would open the engine cover and take a swig from a mickey of whisky he had stored there. Returning to the driver's seat he would reassure the passengers that he had taken care of the problem. He never ceased to be amused by the total absurdity of the sign over his head: YOUR DRIVER: B. DUNN. SAFE, RELIABLE, AND COURTEOUS. It was not long before he lost this job. When the manager of the bus line happened to meet Byron's wife a week later, he shook his head in sympathy, saying, "Mrs. Dunn, you have a problem."

Surprisingly, Byron had a fairly good safety record as a trucker since he usually reserved his drinking binges to the weekends. His home on the outskirts of a small town in the near north was known for its weekend parties. Byron told me that sometimes at the end of a week on the road he would try to sneak out to his place without being seen so that he could get some rest without his drinking buddies crowding into his kitchen. Some of these were off-duty OPP (Ontario Provincial Police) officers. He also spoke of how his poor wife would try in vain to curtail his drinking by finding and confiscating his bottles of whisky and wine or his wallet so that he couldn't buy any more, but she might as well have been trying to stop the earth from turning.

Like many of the truckers of his time, Byron was using bennies (Benzedrine pills) to keep himself going on those long runs with short layovers. (Fortunately, the trucking industry is much better regulated now.) The bennies and the booze were gradually taking their toll on him, and the long hours of driving were causing him back problems with increasing sciatic pain. As a result of all this he was becoming more and more depressed.

One day, in a stupor of depression and drunkenness, Byron took his favourite hunting rifle and walked out to his pickup truck. His wife and daughters took little notice, since this was not the first time they had seen him go hunting when he was drunk. Sitting in his pickup truck Byron loaded the rifle, the same one he had used to kill with a single shot a bear that had been snooping around their back porch. Then, stepping out and standing beside his truck, he raised his head to get the muzzle of the rifle under his chin, his right hand stretching down for the trigger. A moment of hesitation, then POW! In slow motion his body crumpled to the ground. Because he had to raise his head so high, the bullet blew away his face from his chin to just beneath his eyes. He could feel a terrible pain and hear an awful roar in his head so, as far as he could tell, he was not dead yet. Somehow he managed to drag himself to his feet along the side of the truck and then stagger to the house. Stumbling inside he collapsed on the kitchen floor in front of his horrified family.

Byron's next moment of awareness was days later in the Parry Sound Hospital. He could hear the doctor saying to his wife, "There is no way he can make it." No one could get away with telling this seasoned trucker what he could or couldn't do. In that brief moment of consciousness, Byron determined that he *would* make it. If, however, he had known what a long, painful journey it was going to be, he would surely have taken that easy little step into the arms of death waiting at his bedside to embrace him.

When he was discharged from the hospital a couple of months later, there was nothing beneath his sunken eyes but a gaping hole which he kept covered by a large surgical mask. Further restorative surgery was only going to be possible when his condition was more stable. He could not speak, he breathed through a tracheotomy and he could only swallow baby food while lying on his back. He was filled with a confusing mixture of rage, self hatred and depression which he tried to drown in more alcohol. Soon it became clear that he would destroy his family if he continued to live with them, so he began living in boarding houses.

After a couple of years of a terrible descent into ever-greater darkness and confusion, he decided he could stand it no longer. Again he took his rifle, which had a clip of 10 bullets, and he headed for his family home, stopping on the way to buy more bullets. When Byron described this event to me I could see that in his state of depression and drunkenness it was unclear what he was really intending to do once he got home. Parking his truck in front of the house, he got out and fired a few shots into the air. He said that he wanted to see his family one last time before he went somewhere to shoot himself. His wife, hearing the shots and seeing him through the window, must have been terrified. Grabbing the youngest daughter, the only one home at the time, she rushed upstairs into the bathroom at the top of the stairs and locked the door. Since no one came out of the house to greet him, Byron went in. He had already blown his mouth off, so, unable to call out to them, he fired several shots at the door he could see at the top of the stairs. Fortunately, his wife and daughter were far enough away from the door to avoid being shot. They went out through the window and escaped across the field to the neighbour's house. Byron, having emptied the bullets from the clip of his rifle, still wanted to get his wife's attention, as he said, so he set fire to the living room drapes thinking that the smoke would get her to come down. Finally, giving up on a last visit, he drove to the place he had chosen to shoot himself on a dead-end road leading to a river where he used to go fishing. When he got there and tried to reload his rifle, he discovered he had bought the wrong size bullets. Meanwhile, the police were on their way. The OPP, most of them good friends of his, set up a road block on the only way out. Seeing the road block, Byron put the accelerator to the floor and crashed it at high speed, sending him flying through the windshield. He must have had a very powerful guardian angel, for once again he should have died but didn't.

When he recovered enough to leave the hospital he was jailed for attempted murder. He was shocked to discover that his home had burned to the ground. A friend in the OPP convinced him to get a good lawyer, which he did, even though his strongest desire was to die. At the urging of his lawyer he pleaded guilty to the charge in order to avoid the risk of spending the rest of his life in an institution for the criminally insane. The lawyer did well to get him off with a sentence of two years less a day. He was sent to Penetanguishene Institution for the Criminally Insane for an assessment where, as he said, "I was on my very best behaviour that time." A month later he was moved to the Guelph Correctional Centre to finish his sentence.

After 15 months, he appeared before the parole board where he heard the officer say to him, "Well, I suppose you want out of here." Unable to speak, he took his slate and wrote "I don't want out, I want help."

This was the turning point. The medical staff began looking at what could be done to continue the reconstruction of his face. Also, he began speech therapy to learn how to talk again.

A young man, Martin Royackers, as part of his formation as a Jesuit novice, was at that time accompanying Fr. Doug, the prison chaplain. Martin spent considerable time visiting with Byron and playing cards with him. Martin enthusiastically suggested to Doug that Byron was a good candidate for the Farm Community. Doug did not share this enthusiasm, saying, "There is no way we can take that guy; we couldn't possibly handle him." Doug had certainly met and even welcomed into the community very difficult people, but in his opinion Byron topped them all.

There was, for example, James, who had come along a few years earlier. Doug likes to tell the story of how during Holy Week one year, a strange scrawny man with long, scraggly red hair and a sparse beard came into the office in the prison chapel.

He was carrying a box with all his valuables in it, mostly books and papers. He looked comical but very serious when he asked Doug to hold on to his possessions for him. James' instructions were that, in the event of his death, these things were to be distributed to people on a list that he gave to Doug. He then proceeded to say very casually that he was the Son of God and that on one Good Friday he would be killed and that this might be the one.

Well, James didn't die that Good Friday and Doug got to know him quite well. He was serving four years for stealing a police car. The policeman was still in it, asleep on the back seat. James was trying to get away from the Mafia, who he believed were out to kill his family.

Several years before this he had had a "visitation" while working on a garbage truck. He was told that he was the incarnation of Jesus Christ. He tried to enrol in Divinity School, figuring that if he was the Son of God he'd better study theology, but for some reason they turned him down. Since then his life had not been going too well. He was probably happiest in prison, where his divine identity emerged more and more. He introduced himself as Jesus or sometimes as the King. He always signed his name "James the First and Last."

When he was released, James went to live at the Red House. Doug says that it was not easy living with God's son enfleshed in James Steen, but it was never dull. He had a rich and colourful vocabulary and sometimes his conversation was like spoken poetry. At other times he could outdo the vehemence of any Old Testament prophet, especially in the face of blatant disbelief in his divinity. He knew the Psalms and the Gospels by heart, and if he ever made an error while reciting them, as he hitchhiked back and forth across the country, he would ponder long and deep on the significance of the error. He quoted the Scriptures often in reference to himself. He refused to cat apples or any by-product of apples, as they were the occasion of the

Fall. If he discovered he had eaten something with cider vinegar in it by mistake, he would excuse himself and barf it up again.

There were some piglets in the pigpen at that time. One day Doug went out and there was James, in bare feet and with his flaming red hair, sitting in the middle of the pigpen on a boulder, playing the flute to the piglets. They had surrounded him and were jumping up and down in excitement. Another time James was lying on a rubber tube on the pond all afternoon and got burnt to a crisp. He was so burned he couldn't bend his knees, and had to be taken to emergency. Afterwards he said thoughtfully, "I have to speak to my Father about this. We have to do something about Hell."

James had no real followers that we know of, but two elderly sisters of St. Joseph who visited him in prison were considered to be devotees. They were far too gentle and polite to be directly heretical. He called them "the foolish virgins, soon to be wise."

He didn't stay long in the community but went back to his vagabond life. However, once a month or so he would go by the Red House for a few days. He rarely arrived empty-handed, but brought with him wine or a slab of cheese, and once he came with two plump and clucking hens tucked under his arms. He would talk excitedly and tell story after story about his messianic adventures. One time he tried to cross the border and was refused entry into the US. When told that he was an undesirable alien, he said to the customs officers, "Of course I'm undesirable. Have you not read in the Book of Kings, that once you have seen Him, you no longer desire Him?"

A few days before Christmas one year, James arrived and Doug invited him to spend the holidays. James insisted that he had to go to Hamilton, where he would spend Christmas in the Salvation Army Hostel. Doug tried to convince him that a men's hostel would be a lonely place to spend Christmas but he simply asked, "Where else would He spend Christmas?"

James' bodily desires kept betraying his divinity, and he couldn't stand this. He castrated himself, and later tried to cut his penis off and nearly bled to death. Finally he took his own life at his parents' home in Nova Scotia.

He left his Bible at the Red House, in which is inscribed "James the First and the Last." Doug thoughtfully said to me, "I miss his visits, and sometimes I wonder if he were the Christ. I'm glad that I was nice to him."

So Doug was used to welcoming unusual characters, but this guy Byron? However, Martin kept insisting, until finally Doug reluctantly acquiesced, saying, "Okay, we'll give it a try."

After a number of years of Jesuit formation, Martin returned to Guelph and lived in the Farm Community from 1989–1993, where his friendship with Byron continued. During this time Martin was working as a chaplain at Guelph University, but he also did a colossal amount of work on the farm. He had a passion for farm work and in particular for the pigs, having been raised on a pig farm not all that far from Guelph. The same radical compassion in Martin that had brought Byron to the community only deepened during his years of formation. It brought other needy people to the Farm Community, and it led him a few years later to work with poor farmers in Jamaica. There, it seems, his fearless struggle to obtain for the poor land that they justly deserved cost Martin his life at the age of 42. To this day no one has been charged for firing the gun that brought this good man's life to a tragic and far too early end.

Thus, thanks to Martin, when Byron was released from prison on March 19, 1980 he came to live in the Farm House. He probably had only a vague idea of what he was coming to but he really had very little choice. One month later I arrived, thinking I knew what I was coming to and freely choosing to do so. Both of us were in for a few surprises.

★ ★ ★ ★ ★

MEANWHILE, BACK AT THE RANCH

Dear Mum and Dad,

The trees are beginning to turn and we had homemade sausages for supper. We found a mad skunk in the barn and after the autoptician (skunk coroner?) cut off its head with an axe, yes an axe, and then studied its entrails, they found it had rabies. So now we have to kill all the barn cats and we can't sell any cattle for 45 days. I'm going to miss the cats; they always surround me and talk to me while I milk Sheba. I love squirting milk into their faces from her udder and watching them lick each other's faces clean. Wayne wants to put them all in a sack with a big rock and take it out in a canoe and drop it in the middle of the pond. He's got it all planned out. Byron will probably pitchfork them, the way he used to kill the rats before we had cats. Now we will get rats again.

I've been working all day with Harry trying to fix the corn harvester. We're going to get some of the harvesting done by a contractor because we haven't got the people or the equipment to do it all, or rather the psychic energy. We do have the equipment but as all of it needs a lot of repair this is a big load off our collective mind.

Lots of love,
Weesa

5

Shifting Gears

The transition into the Farm Community was probably even more difficult for Byron than for me, although as a trucker he was used to shifting gears. His nerves were shattered, and his battle against depression was to be ongoing for the rest of his life. Only hours after his arrival, on his very first day, he said to Christine with his muffled, raspy voice, "I'm going to kill myself," which might explain why on the way to the house he purchased a knife. Christine, once she was sure she understood what he was saying, in a state of shock and desperation managed to contact the psychiatrist at the mental health clinic with whom Byron had an appointment for the following day. The doctor, however, refused to move the appointment forward, saying only, "Tell Byron I will see him tomorrow." Neither Christine nor Byron got much sleep that night, but Byron did wait to see the doctor, meeting with him several times that week and regularly for the rest of his life.

For his first year with us he still had the tracheotomy, so in order to speak he had to close up the hole in his throat with his fingers. Even then his speech was not clear, and at times was very difficult to decipher. He was a heavy smoker and carried on smoking by sucking on the cigarette through his tracheotomy.

It looked odd but he claimed it gave him a great charge. Little wonder that in later years he suffered from lung cancer.

Since he had no feeling in his lips and only a stub of a tongue, he could not control the steady flow of saliva that trickled out of his mouth. He wore a surgical mask to catch the saliva but also to hide as much of his face as possible. To drink a cup of coffee he would pull down his mask, dump the liquid into his mouth, and then tilt back his head to allow it to flow down his throat, always holding a bunch of napkins or a towel at his chin with the other hand to catch whatever spilled out. He ate lying on his back with a couple of pillows to prop up his head and the plate resting on his chest. So the bedroom was also Byron's dining room. In the beginning he could manage only soft foods but eventually he could chew and swallow a tender steak with the help of a pair of teeth at the back of the left side of his jaw that had survived the accident. He would guide the meat between those two back teeth with his fingers. Salads and most fresh fruit he could not handle. One day, well into his first year with us, Byron was out on a tractor ploughing when suddenly he said to himself, "I don't need this damn mask any more." He tore it off, threw it away and never wore one again.

When he was well, Byron would always rise early. In winter, he began the day by feeding some logs into the wood stove. Over the years he shared with me the secrets of handling this stove, such as learning the differences between the way maple, elm, pine or apple wood burn, and how each burns when dry or when unseasoned; how to get a quick heat in the morning just to take the chill out of the house and how to wiggle in a huge log in the evening that could burn all night. A bond deepened between us through our mutual friendship with this stove. Perhaps it was a residual memory of the kitchen stove in our family home in Oakville that made this one so special for me.

After the morning stove ritual he would sit quietly, sipping a cup of coffee in a leisurely way and then perhaps a second cup. Even in his worst depressions he always began the day in a good mood; then, he told me, the depression would move in like a thick fog in the middle of the morning. So it was always uplifting to be greeted by him first thing in the morning, either in our room or in the cozy kitchen. He would usually come up with some clever remark, such as "Well, today is Monday so the day after tomorrow is Wednesday, the middle of the week, and we haven't done a damn thing yet." Or another favourite: "It's a great day, a great day for a murder." Or he'd recount a story from his years growing up in New Brunswick, such as the one where a neighbour sends her little daughter to the tavern to try to get her drunken father to come home. The child goes to her father and says, "Daddy, daddy, you've got to come quick, the baby calf has fallen into the well." The father, not budging, tells his little girl, "Well, throw it a bale of hay; it's got lots of water."

During the day we would be busy with farm work. When he was well enough, Byron was able to help with the ploughing and other field work as well as take care of the pigs, horses and geese. My specialty was carpentry, with the maintenance and repair of our two barns, and the building and repair of hay wagons and other farm equipment. My oldest brother, Rob, was a carpenter and my brother Gord could fix anything, so as the baby of the family I was always the "gofer." Now I was happy to finally be the one doing the sawing, hammering and fixing. With our 600 acres of mixed farming there was plenty of work for everyone. I also assisted Fr. Doug with the directing of the community, which was primarily the care of people and the leading of worship and other meetings. Not being a social service agency we were able to keep the administrative aspects to a bare minimum. Later, in 1987, I would replace Doug as the community leader.

The farm work was an integral and necessary dimension of the life of the community. We needed the work but we also really needed the produce to sustain our lives. We were able to feed ourselves from the farm as well as market our beef, pork, eggs and other produce. Given the unjust return that farmers receive for their labour, the farm fell far short of enabling the community to be self-sufficient. The Jesuits made a major contribution by making the homes and the land available rent free, as well as offering some direct financial assistance. There was no direct support from government, but those members receiving disability pensions through social services were able to pay some room and board. As the input costs of farming continued to rise, we were forced to do more and more fundraising in order to survive, which in turn gave us an increasing network of devoted friends. It was life-giving for community members to realize that their work was important, and for them to make the link between the work and the food that was put on the table.

The farm was especially a source of healing and restoration for those who, for various reasons, had lost or never experienced the ability or the opportunity to do meaningful work. I could see Byron gaining in self-worth as he experienced the joy and fulfillment of contributing to the farming enterprise, especially in those areas where he was the one responsible for a project or for some of the livestock. For myself, I was discovering that physical work was deeply nourishing for my spirit. The farm provided such a variety of tasks that there was meaningful work for the most limited to the most gifted members, be it the collecting and cleaning of eggs or the running and maintenance of complicated machinery. It was always encouraging to watch how people who had no previous significant work experience began praying for good weather to get in the hay and giving their best effort in the field to make it happen. They would be making the shift from just doing a job to being a part of something they knew to be important, proudly claiming, "This is *our* farm and it's up to us to make it work." The day Mary Makletzoff spent a cold, autumn afternoon at the roadside selling $200 worth of pumpkins she declared with great pride, "If only my psychiatrist could see me now." Much later, under the generous and careful instruction of Don, the farm manager at the time, she even learned to drive a small tractor. She speaks about this experience in an article she was able to write for a Canadian Jesuit magazine, *Compass* (September 1989):

> My first lesson at raking a field was a lot of fun. It sure was exciting for me getting to rake the clean freshly cut hay before it was baled. Don showed me how to put these heavy rakes on and which direction to go in when you are doing it. He showed me what gear to stay in for this field. When I was on my own it felt awesome. I felt like a real worker on the farm. I can get out in a field now and do it without any help. So I am right proud of myself for mastering the art of raking a hayfield.

In this same article Mary Makletzoff writes that "finally after three breakdowns and hospitalizations Ignatius Farm Community is where I ended up. If I was in Toronto right now, I would be either on the street or in a hospital." Mary was perhaps even more proud to have her lengthy article published in a reputable magazine. Giving people a voice was an important aspect of healing and growth.

Michael Mattice came to the community much later, when his foster mother took sick and could no longer care for him. In early childhood he had been rescued by Catholic Children's Aid from terribly abusive alcoholic parents. What Michael lacked in reasoning power was richly compensated for by his great heart and deep faith. He illustrates this same kind of pride about work in an article he wrote himself for *Behind the Barn News,* the community newsletter, on February 14, 1998. It is worth quoting in its entirety:

The Eggs

> Sr. Mary [Schneider] and I did the main barn chores like collecting the eggs and updating the eggs, which are good, cracked or broken eggs but good eggs go into the fridge. If any eggs are cracked then we will put them in this other box.

Any eggs are broken we put them in the container. So the eggs are now updated. Now for the afternoon the eggs must be updated by me or Sr. Mary or Kelly; if any eggs are dirty please report to either me or Kelly straight away as soon as possible. For watering the hens Sr. Mary and Rob make sure that they have good clean water because we don't want to see the chickens getting sick of the dirty water and make sure they get lots of grain. We got the eggs done Sr. Mary and I at the main barn, and she and I will give some water to the chickens at 3.30 and the eggs must be collected and brought up to the shop to be washed and dried and weighed and put into the fridge because if the egg box gets torn then the customer will bring the torn box back to the shop if that one box is torn no customer will buy them: so what we will do is get another box that isn't torn or ruined so that the customer doesn't have to come back to the shop to say that this box is torn or ruined; if the eggs are washed and dried so that the customers don't get sick what my suggestion is that the eggs must and I will repeat again: the eggs must be washed and dried and weighed before the customers buy them. Because if the eggs are not washed and dried and weighed then the customer tends to get sick and that is no good to get sick. So we must wash and dry and weigh them.

Clearly, Michael took his responsibility seriously and knew the importance of working with others.

The teamwork required in much of the work helped to form people to a sense of interdependence and responsibility towards each other. It was healing for those suffering from rejection and isolation to experience the way their activities and attitudes affected others. If one slacked off or pushed too hard, everyone suffered. There were always a few shouting matches and the occasional fight while moving hay bales from the wagons into the barn, as the ones loading them onto the bale elevator might be doing it too quickly for those at the top end stacking them into the loft. It was important to try to get the right combination of people working together, since some had the gift of sowing harmony while for others conflict seemed to be a way of life. Often enough we learned this by our mistakes.

People were welcomed simply as people and not as cases. We did not always know them very well at first, since we did not see it as a good thing to do extensive background checks on those coming to us from prison or psychiatric hospitals or just showing up at the door. Fr. Doug tells the story of Randy, who had been welcomed into the Red House in the early days. We knew he had a painful story, but it was only later that we found out his history. In the middle of the night, Doug kept hearing the basement door banging. Randy was throwing matches, after dripping what he thought was fuel all the way down the stairs and over to the furnace. Fortunately, since he couldn't read very well he had mistakenly used dishwashing detergent. It wasn't flammable, but he thought it was. Shirley was crippled, Aaron was a baby; Doug asked him what would have happened if a fire had started. Randy replied, "Oh, I would have phoned the fire department right away." Then Doug knew it was time for Randy to go, and this was his way of saying it. Randy could not live there, but the Farm Community continued to be his family and the Red House his home. Doug soon learned that Randy had set fires before. The day he was leaving happened to be Dan's birthday. They turned off all the lights and Randy went into the kitchen and lit the birthday candles, all 32 of them. He came in with a glow on his face brighter than all those candles on the cake. Randy loved flames but as far as we know he never lit destructive fires again.

Randy would come for every feast: Christmas, Easter, his birthday. When he first came for Christmas Eve he would go through all the presents and stack all his on one pile. He never opened any until after midnight mass. He would watch TV, waiting by the pile of presents until everyone got back from mass. However, after a couple of years he began bringing gifts: first for Doug, then for the house, then for other people. Then,

Doug said, "The big joy was watching Randy seeing other people opening the gifts he gave. It was great to witness the transformation from selfishness to generosity."

Everyone had a unique gift to contribute to the community, which was sometimes obvious from day one and sometimes took a while to discover. A fellow named Robert, who joined the community later, lived with his parents but came daily to work with us on the Farm. Well, he really did very little work but he was with us. He was quite big and strong but his disability seriously limited his capacity to concentrate and his desire to work. When people were in the garden weeding or picking vegetables, Robert would be happy to sit down in the middle of a row and watch and talk to those doing the work. He would happily carry a heavy basket full of turnips to the shop for one of the women as long as they walked together. Every once in a while Robert might be upset by someone demanding too much of him or for some unknown reason. Then he would no longer be a lad with a disability but a powerful man with a colossal rage and a litany of profanities to go with it. However, when I think of Robert I think mainly of being with him as we all gathered around the table for lunch. It wouldn't be long before he would call my name: "Bill."

"Yes, Robert?"

"I like you."

"I like you too, Robert."

Then, a few minutes later: "Bill."

"Yes, Robert?"

"I like you, Bill."

This little dialogue would be repeated a number of times throughout the meal or at other times during the day with me and with others. Robert's unique gift is like that of God, staying close to us and calling us each by name and reminding us that we are loved. The volunteers enjoyed going into town with Robert because he knew all the cashiers at the stores and many of the clientele, calling each one by name.

Harry, the farm manager, had an infectious sense of humour that was as important as his farming skills. Gordie, on the other hand, with his craziness could push everyone to the edge. Perhaps his gift was to make us turn to each other for support when we found ourselves on that edge. As Byron adjusted to the life and work, his own sense of humour began to blossom and shine for the benefit of all, especially those living with him in the Farm House.

In the evening, after supper and dishes, people were usually free to go their own way. The younger folks in the house tended to gravitate towards the TV. Byron would take longer than the rest to finish eating what was usually his only meal of the day. He rarely watched TV, so he would preside in the kitchen, teaching many of us to play cribbage, a favourite card game. Over the years the two of us played many thousands of crib games. It became a kind of contemplative exercise through which we came to a deep level of communion with only a minimal use of words.

Nights, sharing a room with Byron, were not without drama. With the aid of medication, he would sleep deeply, snoring magnificently as well as talking and walking in his sleep. I would sometimes wake in the middle of the night startled by what sounded like the siren of an ambulance or police cruiser, only to realize that it was just some new notes that Byron's snoring had produced. Eventually, coming to recognize most of the unique sounds he could emit, I would be only rarely startled by them. The sleepwalking was a different story, especially when he couldn't figure out which bed to get back into. Somehow, by the grace of God, these nightly disturbances usually moved me to compassion, so they did not always keep me awake for long. I came to realize that it is not so much noise that keeps us awake, but rather our anger and resentment towards its source.

All in all, those early months were a learning experience for both of us. Sometimes I would find myself staring at Byron's face as he sat on the side of his bed. It reminded me of ancient Greek statues I've seen that have suffered the wear and tear of time: the nose missing, the chin chipped and scarred. Byron's face seemed to have something of that same nobility.

I still remember clearly the day we both happened to be sitting in the little chapel next to our bedroom. Our household had gathered there for a time of reflection, and now everyone had left except the two of us. He turned to me and in his deep, raspy voice mumbled, "You know, I like sharing that room with you." I realized that the feeling was mutual and that what I had most feared in coming to this community, the loss of my privacy, was becoming the greatest gift.

★ ★ ★ ★ ★

MEANWHILE, BACK AT THE RANCH

Farm House Tales

By Louisa Blair (Weesa)

After lunch Wayne and I drag the air hose and compressor down to the barn to clean out the pit under the cattle weigh scale.

"Fucking Hussein fucking pansy left me to do it myself. I'll kill him, the fucking Paki pansy," says Wayne.

The boards are off the pit, that's as far as they have got after a whole morning's work. It is half full with liquid manure. We set about scooping it out with buckets, taking turns carrying them out into the yard and emptying them. The cattle stand and watch us with their heads slightly lowered. After a while Wayne only wants to carry, not scoop. Scooping means you're up to your knees in manure.

"Okay, carry then," I say. But soon he doesn't even want to carry anymore.

"I'll just put it back here," he says, and pours a full bucket back into the pit.

"What the fuck did you do that for," I ask, and he smiles.

"Just to see you mad." I pull myself upright to look at him, and hate him intensely. I keep working a while longer while he fiddles with the electric cattle prod that hangs on the wall behind me. Finally I have the pit clean enough to air-hose.

"You do that," I say to Wayne, handing him the hose while I search the floor of the pit for the board screws. My head is rammed against the side of the pit as I feel around in the thick silt at the bottom. Wayne suddenly shoves the hose in my ear and squirts a jet of cold air into it. Then he gives this huge laugh, the laugh he uses on a Saturday morning when he is watching the wrestling on TV and sees someone getting his head stamped on.

"FUCK OFF! What the fuck are you doing, you asshole!" I yell, jumping out of the pit. Wayne follows me, laughing, as I drag the compressor back up to the shop. He is dancing rings around me, his great belly shoved out in the vest with the oil stains.

"I wanted to see if you could swear," he said.

"Well, now you know," I said primly.

The last time I saw Wayne he was living in protected housing at Sherbourne and Dundas [in Toronto]. I went in and he gave me his huge affectionate hug, his belly shoving me backwards, and held me a long time, always too long. He had three rows of chairs and sofas lined up as in a theatre, and facing them two 28-inch TVs on coffee tables. They were each set on a different channel. "I can watch my soaps and a movie at the same time," he said proudly.

In the corner of the room was his bed, with a Sally-Ann blanket. In the kitchen he was raising fish.

"I got these tanks in Woodstock," he said. "This here is a breeding tank." A pot of fish food stood among an open can of beans on the counter. He showed me the bathroom, too. He was using the bathtub as storage space. He picked up a pile of blankets.

"These are them I was talking about," he said. "They are from the Fred Victor Mission when it closed. Do you need them?"

"Yes, please," I said. I did need them. I had just moved to Toronto and I had nothing but a bag of clothes. He also gave me a coffee table that he said he didn't need. I still have these possessions, and I cherish them. Love, Bill always said, is giving someone the right to be generous.

6

If I Wasn't Here, I'd Be Dead

It was one thing to have acknowledged the gift of sharing the room with Byron; it was quite another thing to continue living out this gift day to day. We had begun a journey that would take us over some rough roads and through some long, dark tunnels as well as through some fascinating landscapes, a journey that would be rarely boring, a journey with plenty of laughter and more than a few tears.

During the community meeting in which Byron summed up his understanding of our vision in his blunt, shocking way – "If I wasn't here, I'd be dead" – I immediately grasped both the meaning of our community and the pain and precariousness of his life. It was at that time that I began praying that his life not come to a violent end. On more than one occasion it looked to me as if that prayer request was not going to be fulfilled.

The early months were a time of adjustment for the two of us as well as for the entire household. We had moved into a life that seemed to be always teetering on the edge of disaster. Sr. Christine, whose previous mission had been teaching and, for a short period of time, the Mistress of Novices for the Loreto Sisters, was clearly making good use of her gifts in this new mission. Her strong personality along with her desire and ability to care for others with little concern for her own needs were the only structure that seemed to be holding the place together. She was thriving on the energy it took to be constantly trying to put order into the chaos. The house had officially opened on the feast of Epiphany, the Christian celebration of the revelation of God in the Christ child to the nations, represented by the Magis from the East following the star to the stable of Bethlehem. This was an appropriate starting date for this home, where we were to be constantly surprised by manifestations of the divine in the most unlikely and messy aspects of our lives together.

Since Christine, Byron and I were all about the same age, we tended to get on well together and in different ways were forced into parental roles in relationship to the younger members of the household. Larry, the youngest of the group, was the first to arrive from the Correctional Centre, but within a few days disappeared. He reappeared a week later with his feet blistered and bloody from having walked all the way from his hometown, Chatham, well over 200 kilometres. Larry was very much like a wild animal in search of food, a food that would nourish his desperate, unnamed longing to claim his manhood and its meaning. There was no one who packed his belongings more often than Larry. He would leave almost every other week but would return a day or two later. When he stole money from us he would usually bury it somewhere, such as beside the Bowlerama or in the flowerbed outside the bus depot. I can remember walking down in the ditch along the highway looking for the credit cards of a distinguished British Catholic theologian and writer who was visiting at the time. We found the wallet and the cards, and Larry promised to pay back the twelve dollars he had quickly spent in the hotel where he often went to watch the strippers. The other $10 he dug up and returned.

An old workshop had been fixed up behind the house where Larry could play his music as loud as he liked. One night in a fit of anger he went out there and smashed and tore up everything: his stereo, records, magazines as well as the windows and door.

Byron was immensely patient with Larry, who may have reminded him of one of the wild horses back in New Brunswick that he had tried to tame enough for his dad to trade or sell. (Well, maybe not, because he wasn't very patient with our horses.) He reached the limit of his patience the night he heard a crash at the bedroom window, and came charging out, still pulling on his pants, looking for a two-by-four to start whacking whoever was out there. He was stunned to find the rest of us sitting calmly at the kitchen table while Larry raced around the house tearing off all the screens.

One night when Larry failed to come home, Christine and I went around to all the bars at one in the morning looking for him. Christine said it was the first time she'd been in all those bars late at night, but it certainly would not be the last time. Since we did not find him, we informed the police. Later that morning they found him asleep on a park bench close to the home of a friend of the community, a woman on whom Larry had a crush. Christine and I went to collect him. He had overdosed on pills, stolen from another member of the community, so we had to put his arms over our shoulders and practically carry him out to the car. A woman standing on the sidewalk watching us was shaking her head in obvious disgust as we dragged our scruffy "son" out of the police station. Byron got a great chuckle out of the whole affair.

People like Larry did not always help our relationship with Loyola House, the retreat centre that was on the same property. Men and women came to this centre for periods of a few days, a week or even a month to live an experience of prayer, contemplation and personal renewal in an atmosphere of solitude. One or two of the Jesuits working in the centre had expressed reservations about the Farm Community and whether it would be safe to have these people around. There was a 30-day retreat going on, and the retreatants were beginning the fourth week of this experience; that is to say, they were beginning to pray with the mystery of the resurrection of Jesus. A Sister who was making this retreat under the direction of one of these Jesuits decided to go into the nearby Jesuit graveyard to start her day with the rising sun before a statue of Jesus. It was a warm spring day, very misty. The previous night Larry had come to the graveyard after an incident at the Farm House where he got very angry and stormed off. He was sleeping on a bench not far from this statue. The Sister, standing between the bench and the statue, was praying there, preparing to greet the risen Jesus. The mist started to lift and she turned around just as Larry, with scraggly beard and long, dishevelled hair started to get up from the bench. The poor woman ran out of the garden terrified – not like Mary Magdalene with good news to announce to the disciples but rather with bad news for her director about the strange man in the graveyard. She had failed to see the risen Lord in the person of Larry, who had been just as surprised and upset as she had been.

While I'm on the subject of our relationship to the retreat centre, there is another incident that's worth telling here. We had a man in the community by the name of Robert Lee, who was being angered and frustrated by some beavers who kept building a dam on a stream that ran under a culvert on the road behind the Farm House. Every morning Robert Lee would find the culvert blocked by the beaver dam and the road flooded. Every day he would work feverishly to remove the dam to allow the stream to flow freely through the culvert. The next morning the dam would be reconstructed and the road flooded. Robert, a man of tremendous determination, was not going to be beaten by a few "damn vermin." After several days of this frustrating exercise he decided to make a scarecrow, or rather a scarebeaver, which he propped up on an old pitchfork in the middle of the stream in front of the culvert. It looked like a real man, complete with plaid shirt, overalls and straw hat. Well, to everyone's amazement it worked. The beavers were scared off and gave up their damn dam project. We left the scarebeaver there in the stream and eventually forgot about it. Months passed and eventually it fell face down into the stream and lay there, letting the water run over it and silt build up on it. It never occurred to anyone to remove it from the stream. One day a Sister who was making a retreat at the centre came for a walk and stopped to pray there on the road above the culvert. Her prayerful reverie came to a shocking halt when she looked down and saw the body lying there half buried in silt in the bed of the stream. The director of the retreat centre let us know in no uncertain terms that we had some cleaning up to do.

One Wednesday evening in the Farm House, Gordie failed to come for the house meeting. He was up in the bathroom, where he usually spent two hours or more at a time. When Christine checked out the bathroom later she discovered a huge hole in the wall.

"Gordie, what happened?" she asked.

"I fell," replied Gordie. "But don't worry, I'll fix it with chicken wire."

At another house meeting Gordie said, "I don't know who's putting all these dirty thoughts in my head, but I wish they'd stop!"

"Gordie," I said, "you may have dirty thoughts in your head, but none of us are putting them there," at which point Byron announced, "There's a terrific war over in Spain."

Gordie was not with us for very long. On the weekends he sometimes went to visit his sister in another town. One Monday after such a visit the police came and took him away. He had committed a crime while he was away that landed him back in prison, the one place structured enough for him to feel safe.

Aidan was the first volunteer to arrive to be a support to Christine when she opened the Farm House. He might have been second in command, except that there was really no second with Christine at the helm, and his gifts were not in the area of leadership. Aidan, then in his mid-30s, had come over from Ireland some years earlier with a rock band. Before coming to the Farm House he had worked at odd jobs, but his energies had gone mainly into being a drummer and singer with the band. He was a man of faith, and came here out of a desire to deepen his commitment to the Catholic Church. He found a very different kind of Catholicism than the traditional Irish faith he had been used to, but he was not disappointed. Our worship services usually took place in the living room with a coffee table for an altar. Community members participated more fully than was possible in a church setting. The homilies were often community sharings, and Doug and I always emphasized the love and compassion of God. There was no talk of hell and damnation, since most of our people had already heard more than enough condemnation.

Not being very robust, Aidan had good reason to be a bit wary of Larry and Gordie. Well, I suppose we were all frightened of Gordie, who was full of rage and totally unpredictable. One afternoon, Dougie happened to walk into the hayloft just as Gordie, with a pitchfork, was heading for Aidan. Dougie's surprise appearance broke the tension and Gordie dropped his weapon. There is no telling what would have transpired if Dougie hadn't shown up at that moment, but Aidan is convinced that he owes his life to Dougie.

Aidan would have been more in his element in the world of music, but the life here was a growthful challenge for him and, being a responsible person as well as a pretty good cook, he was able to make a significant contribution to the community.

He remains grateful to this day for all that he gained from the three years he lived with us. Byron, who loved to tease, took special delight in teasing Aidan. Aidan might come in from the farm and ask, "Where's Christine?" Without a moment's hesitation Byron would respond, "She's up tarrin' the roof" or "You know that grocery store down on Woodlawn Avenue where she goes to shop? Well…she's not there."

As Byron adjusted to the people and the environment, he began to get more in touch with himself and his own inner pain and loss. For the past three years his addictions had been controlled by incarceration, but now this control was gone. It was not long before he began to numb himself with excessive doses of medications that he would store up for several days in order to be able to take them all at once. When he became more mobile, especially after he bought himself a second-hand pickup truck, he began resorting to his favourite escape: alcohol. That little black Mazda 150 may have brought some independence and satisfaction into his life, but it certainly brought a great deal of grief as well.

The first indication of storm clouds on the horizon appeared one summer evening during our first year. I was sitting in our prayer room writing my journal when Byron passed through, holding a letter and on the verge of tears. He told me he was going into town. I followed him into our room to talk with him. A friend had written to say that he presumed Byron knew that one of his daughters was getting married the next day. Since this was his oldest daughter, she was the one he knew best and held dearest to his heart. It pained him deeply not to have been informed and not to be able to be there for the wedding. He was determined to go into town for the night to get drunk. I tried in vain to dissuade him. This was especially difficult for me, since I was about to leave for the airport to fly to Victoria, British Columbia, to preach a retreat in the William Head prison. I tried to convince him to come to the airport with me and Lorraine, who was driving me there. Lorraine, a friend of the community who came often to visit, was a good friend of Byron's and perhaps something of a daughter to him. In any case, Lorraine was far more forceful and determined than I, and finally between the two of us we managed to get him to change his mind and come with us to the airport. At the airport he promised not to start drinking while I was away, which brought tears to my eyes as I gave him a farewell hug. During my absence Byron rented a car and went with Dougie on a trip to the north in the area of his hometown – something he needed to do even though it probably deepened his pain and sense of loss.

For weeks afterwards he battled with deep depression and finally went into Homewood, the local psychiatric hospital, to get professional help. When he returned to the house three weeks later he was at least able to manage his depression with an increase of medication. This helped to get him through another crisis a couple of months later, when he got notice that his wife was filing for divorce. He could accept the inevitability of this, but it grieved him deeply. Even after that I still never heard him speak a negative word about this woman who had given him "three lovely daughters" and who for years had put up with his often outrageous behaviour.

In November, Joe Guitar arrived from the Correctional Centre to live with us and to push us to the limits of our patience. He was a scrappy little guy with a drinking problem that was out of control. This was the fellow who would take his aggression out on the cows when he thought no one was watching. On the day he arrived he spent only a couple of hours in the house before going into town to get drunk and then came staggering back at midnight as sick as Luke the Red House dog would be after getting into rotting food in the compost heap. Joe was about the last person on earth that Byron would have befriended under normal circumstances but it wasn't long before Joe's drinking got Byron going. Together they went into town one day but only Joe came back, so drunk he could hardly walk or talk. Byron had bought a stock of booze and gone to a motel. The next afternoon Byron showed up with Joe in a rented car, prepared to go north. Christine and I got into the car with them and finally managed to talk him into returning the car and going instead to a motel just down the street. We booked him into the nearby Woodlawn Motel, taking into his room from the trunk of the car two cases of beer and a gallon of wine. Half an hour later, when I returned to the motel with some food for him, it was fortunate the door was unlocked because he was already so drunk he could not get to his feet. I wanted to weep and I wanted to punch him in the face, but I just dropped the things on the table and left.

Dougie was very sullen and upset when I got back to the house. When I asked what was bothering him it came pouring out: "I don't know how you can be so soft on that dirty, drunken bastard. I would have booted his ass so hard he'd never come back."

Dougie, a big, strong 19-year-old, had come to us just after Aidan, also to be a support to Christine. He had asked about joining the Jesuits but was told he was not ready for this and that perhaps the Farm Community could help him mature. His vision and pedagogy about running the Farm House were often at odds with Christine's and mine, and with two of the community's fundamental ways of proceeding: "unconditional acceptance" and "non-punishment." The unconditional acceptance of persons did not imply accepting all of their behaviour, but sometimes it seemed best even to accept some outrageous behaviour as a way of assuring the person that they were totally accepted. Gradually, as trust deepened, they could be challenged.

Dougie wasn't into subtle distinctions. He believed that punishment could go a long way towards correcting unacceptable behaviour. There were times when I wondered if maybe he was right and I was just enabling Byron to persist in unhealthy ways of functioning. It was not always clear to me whether I was acting out of community principles or my own fear of confrontation and conflict. This was a doubt and uncertainty that would plague me for years to come.

The following evening, when I went to the motel to see how Byron was doing, I was pleasantly surprised to find him in fairly good shape, considering how much alcohol he had consumed. Trusting his promise to come home the next morning early before the banks opened, I paid for one more night there. Later that evening, sitting at the kitchen table in the Farm House with Dougie and Fr. Doug, I spoke about my visit with Byron. Dougie exploded again: "I can't believe you're still wasting your time with that goddam bastard. He ought to go back to jail where he belongs."

"You don't know what the hell you're talking about," I sputtered, just as angrily. "You don't have the faintest idea what he's going through. You, you..." I was at a loss for words, but it didn't matter because Dougie was already stamping out, heading up to his room.

Fr. Doug helped me to calm down and encouraged me to go talk with Dougie. When I went into his room he burst into tears; then we were able to begin an honest conversation. He spoke about the bad day he had had in Toronto visiting doctors and not getting good reports on his health and about his fears with respect to all this. We talked about his feelings towards Byron and his drinking but did not get to the issue of Dougie's relationship to his own family and if this could be influencing his present feelings. Nor was I ready to talk about my family story and how that could be influencing my dealings with Byron.

As a young boy, one of the reasons I enjoyed using the sunroom addition to our little house for sleeping was that it enabled me to listen in on the adult conversations taking place in the kitchen between my parents and with their guests. One night I overheard my dad speaking with Mom about her drinking, saying that he regretted and blamed himself for introducing Mom to alcohol. This wasn't so much a fight or an argument, but more just the painful recognition of a serious problem. If my mom said anything in response, I didn't hear it or didn't retain it. It seems that until then I had not been aware that Mom had a drinking problem. My feeling was mostly one of great sadness, which seems to be precisely what Dad was feeling and expressing. I have never been sure of all that was at the root of Mom's drinking. I know that there was insecurity around the shortage of money and having to raise four young children, often very much alone since Dad's work took him away regularly for anywhere from a week to 10 days. He was on the road more than he was home. Being a minority in a mainly white town would have added to her isolation and loneliness.

In the months and years that followed I did become increasingly aware of the cases of beer that would stack up in the coal shed and Mom's growing anxiety around feeding her addiction and getting rid of the evidence. Until I reached my late teens I did not detect any notable diminishment in Mom's ability to care for her family and household. She always kept her children, her home and herself neat and clean. In retrospect I can see how joy was slowly being drained out of her life.

After we moved back to Toronto, Mom's addiction started to have more noticeable effects. I was with her one day when she seemed to me to be in a kind of trance, taking me by the hand and leading me out the side door and down the driveway, saying, "Come on, come on" but unable to respond to my questioning where we were going. After a few steps she fell to the ground with a seizure. Fortunately, Dad was home at the time and could take charge of the situation, but I was very frightened. Even more worrisome and frightening was the time she just disappeared for three days, finally calling to say she was in Buffalo, and asking Dad to come and get her. I know the situation deeply troubled Dad, but except for the occasional argument it was rarely the source of any obvious division. If it was more than this, they certainly managed to keep it between themselves.

I was often home alone with my folks since my sister was in residence studying nursing at St. Joseph's Hospital and my brothers were in relationships that would lead to marriage. One day I left the house to go play baseball but had only gone a few steps when I realized I had forgotten my baseball glove and dashed back to get it. I burst into the house to the surprise of seeing my dad sitting on the chesterfield on which my Mom was stretched out with her head in his lap as he caressed her face and they looked lovingly into one another's eyes. First, I was shocked to realize that they had been eagerly waiting for me to leave the house so that they could be alone like this. Later, as I had time to think about it, my shock turned to delight in the awareness of the unsuspected affection they had for each other. It seemed that the primary way Dad was dealing with Mom and her drinking was just to keep on loving her in a gentle way. He wasn't into tough love.

As a family we were not great at verbalizing our difficulties or at challenging and confronting one another which, I suppose, could have added to the length of years that Mom lived with her drinking problem. On the other hand, our care for her perhaps helped her to function as well as she did in spite of her addiction. It was only after Dad died suddenly of a heart attack in 1963 that Mom really lost control of herself. I was away in Europe during Mom's worst years and only learned of this later through my brothers and sister. I was saddened but also relieved not to have been more present to Mom and the rest of the family during those difficult years. In any case, my approach with Byron and his drinking was obviously shaped by more than just the Farm Community vision.

I was beginning to realize that this community had some striking differences from my family and from family in general. We all came to the community from such very different backgrounds, differences that were deeply rooted in us from our earliest childhood and shaped by radically different life experiences. While I tended to avoid and minimize conflict, others seemed to thrive on it. While I was predisposed to trust, others for very good reasons were almost incapable of trust. Some, like me, freely chose the community, but some came out of desperation, with few other options. A few were sent by the courts and could hardly wait until their time of parole ended so that they could leave. The differences made living together very difficult, but were also a source of richness and strength.

For those of us who chose to come and saw ourselves more in a helping role, we faced the challenge of loving and accepting people whose loveableness was not always evident. In family there is a predisposition towards accepting and loving each other. You want to and almost have to love your parents and siblings. In community, when people drive us up the wall it can take a mammoth effort not to drive them through the wall. This is where we discover how much we need the help of God and one another. The strength of community is that we can support each other in this challenge. When Dougie wanted to kick Byron in the ass, I was there to talk with him about another way. When I wanted to smash Byron in the face, Doug or Christine were there to help me find another way. Some were better at confrontation, others better reconcilers and peacemakers.

For those who came out of desperation and need, it was often a healing experience for them to be able to reach out and support others that were just as needy or even more so than themselves. Byron grew in his exercise of fatherhood towards Larry and others. The gentleness and simplicity of Bob and Julie called forth unsuspected tenderness in him. Mary

Makletzoff helped us all to laugh and be playful, at least on her good days. Her bad days were something else.

It seems that at an early age I had learned to avoid or suppress my inner pain, unlike Byron and a number of others in the community for whom the pain was too great to hide and was always close to the surface. Not many years ago I was at a weekend formation session for pastoral ministers working with l'Arche communities. During a session on grieving we were asked to write down and then share in small groups about three grief experiences in our lives, including one from our childhood. I couldn't think of one from my childhood, so in desperation I wrote "leaving Oakville to move back to Toronto." I had no idea why this came to mind since I was not aware of any grief attached to this experience. It is true that I had dearly loved life in Oakville. The pressure to return to Toronto came from my brothers and sister, who had begun socializing with the black community there. Not yet into dancing and dating, my socializing all centred around sports but, nevertheless, I made the move easily, enthusiastically taking up sports in my new surroundings, Riverdale Collegiate and the Coxwell-Danforth neighbourhood. So, when in the small group we began sharing our grieving experiences, I was hoping we would run out of time before I had to share my childhood experience of grief, since I could think of nothing to say about this move from Oakville to Toronto. But, alas, we did not run out of time. Finally, it was my turn. I was feeling really silly sharing something so meaningless, but when I came out with the words "moving from Oakville to Toronto," to my utter amazement I burst into deep sobbing. In retrospect I can see that there was a painful uprooting that took place there. By the time of the move I had a number of very good friends. At the Oakville-Trafalgar High School I was a popular, successful student and athlete. I loved living on the edge of this small town where I was close to nature; the trees, the fields and the lake were like intimate friends.

I was leaving all this for the big city of Toronto: a frightening, confusing, lonely place.

This whole experience made me wonder: if there was so much pain hidden under such a seemingly gentle event, how much more pain was I holding some place deep inside me? In any case, within the community some pain was simply unavoidable and insuppressible even for me.

Christine and I picked up Byron the next morning and brought him home, where he spent the next few days sleeping and being sick. It took him over a week to recover, and it took me even longer. I had to come to a new level of acceptance that the journey with this roommate of mine was not going to be an easy ride.

* * * * *

MEANWHILE, BACK AT THE RANCH

Dear Mum and Dad,

I have been booted out of my room as it is being fixed up so that I will no longer be poisoned by the urea formaldehyde insulation. Just about all the vehicles on the farm have broken down and getting supplies by foot isn't easy. Then Byron got drunk yesterday and quite aggressive and eventually we took him to a motel to finish his whisky. It breaks my heart when he does that. Each time I am sadder, the more I know and love him. Then Shirley beat up Barbara at the Red House last night. There's a full moon, Bill is away, and things seem to fall apart when he goes.

Love from
Weesa

7

One for the Jack

Cribbage, the card game I learned from Byron in the first months of our time together, became an important part of the social life of the community and a kind of sacrament of our friendship.

I might have come back from doing the chores in the barn on a Saturday afternoon and found Byron in the sunroom, the multi-windowed room we created by closing in the back porch. He would have been sitting in his favourite chair, a swivel rocker with dark green upholstery, now black along the front edge of the seat cushion, crusted with layers of Byron's saliva and spilled coffee. An area of the carpet just in front of his chair had suffered the same fate. Both chair and carpet were scarred by cigarette burns, little reminders that Byron Dunn slept here. He loved to sit there basking in the sun, when there was any, where he could turn to the left and look out at the pasture and swamp beyond it, or turn even farther and check out the transport trucks coming and going along Highway 6, which runs from Hamilton to Tobermory. Looking straight ahead he could oversee all that went on in this long, narrow room, an alternate place for people to relax and socialize free from the sounds and images of the TV. With a slight turn to the right he could see through the door leading into the kitchen, and by leaning forward check out the comings and goings through the door on the far side of the kitchen through which everyone passed to enter or leave the house.

Beginning to shuffle the deck of cards he had picked up from the crib board that always sat on the little table between his chair and his opponent's chair, he said, "Come on." As I sat down, he slammed the deck on the board and cut off the top third of the cards, lifting them to reveal the bottom one, which turned out to be a two of diamonds. This drew a smile from him, since the person with the lowest card gets to deal first, a definite advantage in this game. I cut the remainder of the deck and, to my delight, turned up an ace. Taking up the deck to shuffle and deal, I smiled at him and sang "Na na na na na." To which he responded, "Don't count your chickens before they're hatched, Clarke." The game was on.

While dealing the cards, I informed him of the latest news from the farm: "We had another calf born today – a beautiful, big heifer."

"How many more to come?" he asked.

"This one was number 31, so there are seven more to finish the spring calving. I think there are 34 expected for the fall."

At this point we became silent to examine our six cards and decide which two to throw into the crib hand. This was an easier decision for me since the dealer gets to count the crib hand as well as his own, but nevertheless Byron was first to discard his two into the crib. As I continued to hesitate about which way to split my cards, Byron said, "There's probably a few more calves born by now." I got the hint and dropped two cards into the crib so the game, as well as the farm update, could proceed.

Byron cut the remainder of the deck, which turned up a seven of diamonds, and then he played a seven of clubs from his hand, saying, "See one, play one," then going on to ask, "How's Babes doing?" Babes, the mare Byron had purchased some time earlier, was good company for Patches, an older horse given to the community by friends who were moving from their country home into the city. Riding was a new experience for me but I found it a good way to be with Byron, who seemed to especially enjoy trying to teach me the secrets of showing a horse who's boss. The horses certainly respected him as boss, but I doubt if they delighted in seeing him come into the barn to saddle them. I cringed for the poor horses at the way Byron kneed them in the belly to knock the air out of them so he could get the girth good and tight. Babes was not that young either, but Byron had her bred in the fall and was eagerly waiting for her to foal.

"As far as I know, Babes is fine. Fifteen for two," I said firmly as I played an eight of hearts.

"Twenty-four for three," he proclaimed, completing the run of seven and eight with a nine of clubs.

"Thirty for four" was my eager response, playing a six of spades to continue the run.

Byron flashed a look of disgust that immediately shifted to satisfaction as he threw down an ace of clubs: "Thirty-one for two."

This walnut-stained board was several times larger than the normal crib board, being about three feet long and almost a foot wide. It was a gift to Byron from Fr. Doug, who "borrowed" it from the Jesuit Community at Ignatius College, situated nearby on this same property. Doug would have figured that his fellow Jesuits, being a diminishing number with less and less time or interest in playing cards, could not match Byron's appreciation for this fine crib board. With his many years of chaplaincy service at the correctional centre, Doug had acquired certain affinities with the men he served. A friend aptly said of him, "He has the mind of a criminal, and the heart of a saint."

I then played a three of diamonds and Byron played an eight of clubs.

"Fifteen for two and one for the last card," I said smugly, playing a four of hearts.

Then Byron counted the total of points in his four cards plus the seven of diamonds that was the cut card, a good cut for him that gave him several multiples adding up to 15, each worth two points, and then a couple of runs of three, plus the four clubs, for a total of 16 points. It was his turn to be smug as he moved his red peg along the board well ahead of my blue, perhaps remembering as he did his times from his trucking days when he stepped on the gas to pass a buddy of his roaring along the 401 highway. I counted seven points in my hand, moving my blue peg up the board after his red. Then I turned over the crib hand to count, which had the king and five which I put in, and a king and a 10 that Byron had thrown in. "Thanks, Pal," I smiled at him as I counted: "Fifteen for two, 15-four, 15-six, and two for the pair makes eight," and eased my blue peg three points into the lead.

The next couple of hands were poor for both of us, which made us less interested in the cards and freer to chat about other things. He told me about a time when as kids, he and his friends were fooling around in the snow with a frozen cat they had discovered. Later, an irate neighbour woman came after them, asking, "Who hit my Johnnie with a froze tomcat?"

As I went for a drink of water the phone rang. It was pushed almost off the back of the little table in the corner by the crib board. Byron answered it; something he would not have done in the early months of his time with us. This changed the day he went to the barn behind the Farm House to feed his geese, and discovered that a bunch of goslings had hatched. With childlike excitement he came running up to the house to share his good news, and since there was no one home at the time he picked up the phone and called Fr. Doug at the Red House. That was the first time he had used the phone since he shot himself, and it freed him to continue using it.

As I returned with my cup of water, Byron handed me the phone, with a look of patient sympathy, having recognized the voice of a frequent caller. I took the receiver and said "Hello," and then "Uh-huh, uh-huh," at 30-second intervals for the next 10 minutes, with the phone between my shoulder and ear and proceeding with the crib game. Finally, I said to the caller, "I'm sorry, I have to go now…you're welcome…yes, you're welcome…yes…thanks for calling." Byron, resigned to this kind of interruption, made no comment as I apologized to him. A few minutes later he repeated a favourite line of his from a Jim Reeves song: "Put your sweet lips a little closer to the phone."

When phone calls like this interrupted a cribbage game or whatever else I might be doing, it would have been more honest and respectful to tell the caller that we could reconnect later rather than to give them only my divided attention. However, the time and effort it took to make a new connection often seemed like adding one more burden and demand on my limited time. Finding the balance between my friendship with Byron, other friendships both inside and outside of the community, my relatives, and my ministry of spiritual accompaniment with a number of people and my commitment and responsibilities to the whole Farm Community was a constant juggling act. This meant that at times I was not adequately present to any one of them. Given my passive nature I tended to respond to the immediate claim rather than plan and organize for the most creative use of my time and energy. Jesuit spirituality encouraged me to do the latter, that is, with inner freedom always to make choices in the light of what is discerned as being more conducive to the praise and glory of God, but all too often my own limitations and selfishness got in the way of the ideals proposed by our founder, St. Ignatius. Since Byron was always right there with a large claim on my attention, the scale often tipped in his favour. Certainly there was a lack of freedom and an exclusiveness in my friendship with him that in some ways was detrimental to community life and at times hurtful to others. My early Jesuit formation had warned of the dangers of "particular friendships," but by this time I was well aware that the greater danger for us as celibates was loneliness. This was a much needed relationship that anchored me deeply in the community and kept me going for the long haul. Without it I may not have survived.

The game started to heat up as we rounded the bend at the end of the board and were neck and neck (or fender to fender) in the home stretch. It was once again my deal, which meant I had two hands to count against Byron's single hand, but Byron got to count first. We both needed 17 points to go out, with the odds in my favour, and yet Byron, as always, acted as if he was in full control, true to one of his favourite sayings: "Come big or stay home." We were both completely focused on the game, so that when Mary Makletzoff came in and asked, in her deep voice that often had an angry edge, who was winning and then described in great detail the chocolate cake she was going to bake for Sunday dinner, and the number of eggs she collected that morning, and the colour of the new calf, and, and...., we didn't pay her much attention, which didn't discourage her lively monologue. Byron, chuckling with the memory of his earlier story, repeated, "Who hit my Johnnie with a froze tomcat?"

I played my cards as cautiously as I could but he outplayed me to peg four points, so that as he prepared to count his hand he needed 13 points to go out. I still needed 17, but with 14 points in my hand I figured there should be at least three in the crib to put me over the finish line – that is, if Byron couldn't make it. The cut was a three of hearts and he had a pair of fives, and a pair of Jacks, which he counted: "15 for two, 15–four, 15–six, 15–eight, and a pair is 10, and another pair is…one dozen roses." His red peg stopped right at the line, and it looked as though he hadn't made it, but just as I began to smile, we both noticed that one of his Jacks was a heart, the same suit as the cut, so it was his turn to smile, as he announced triumphantly, "and one for the Jack."

As the loser, I quickly grabbed up the cards and began shuffling for the next game. Byron hesitantly accepted Mary's offer to make him a coffee. Mary, an energetic woman in her early 30s who was delightful even when angry, did everything in a mad rush, so Byron was never sure whether there would be half or two and a half teaspoons of instant coffee in his cup, nor just how much cream and sugar. Since Mary's arrival, his early morning time of stillness had not been the same. Mary was also an early riser, and in her generosity insisted on making coffee for him. He was amazingly patient with Mary's intrusive presence, and without any sign of dissatisfaction, gratefully took whatever he got by way of a coffee. Mary's father was a Russian nobleman, so she thrilled to hear us call her the Russian Princess, even though we were usually thinking *rushin'* princess.

Game two proceeded with a few interruptions. Byron paused periodically to drink his coffee. Holding a bunch of tissue to his chin, he tilted back his head and gently poured coffee into his mouth a little at a time. The quickly saturated tissues didn't quite catch all that spilled out in the process. Once the coffee was finished it was time for a cigarette. Now that his tracheotomy was closed, he smoked in the normal way, except that he needed to use the fingers of both hands to close his lips around the cigarette, which was a bit of a trick while lighting up without a third hand to hold his Zippo lighter. He took great pleasure in both the coffee and the cigarette.

Luck was on my side in this next game as the good cards kept coming to me and the poor ones to him. After getting yet another poor hand, he shook his head and said, "There's hard times in the Maritimes." Once while he was dealing he winked at Tom, who had appeared in the doorway from where he could see my cards and was making signs to Byron about what he was seeing. Tom came to the community about the same time as me, starting out in the Red House but then moving here to the Farm House. He was a huge man, well over six feet tall and 250 pounds. The size of his large head was magnified by his abundant, thick black hair and bushy beard and moustache. His very imposing figure would have been frightening if it weren't for the kind brown eyes that revealed his gentle spirit. This doorway was Tom's roost where he loved to just park himself, filling almost the entire space, and from there observing everything that went on in the room. Byron was very good with Tom, pulling him out of his fearful shyness and encouraging his spirit of playfulness.

Both Tom and I for our first day of work on the farm were sent to the garden to thin the carrots. It was pitiful to watch this huge man with hands like bunches of bananas trying to get a hold of every other tiny carrot top. It wasn't long before he gravitated from garden work towards driving tractors.

Tom had one great passion: mashed potatoes. Anyone in the community who could cook mashed potatoes well was a friend of Tom's, providing they knew enough to set aside at least a pound of them just for him, along with a quarter pound of margarine (for me mashed potatoes and margarine will always be measured in pounds not kilos). It was not high-energy food, but that suited him just fine. The one area where Tom exhibited high energy was in the bathroom off the kitchen not more than six feet from the end of the kitchen table. He had a nervous bowel that propelled him into the bathroom as soon as he finished stashing away his pound and a quarter of mashed potatoes and margarine and whatever else had been piled onto his plate. Unfortunately, the rest of us were still eating when the thunder began rattling the flimsy bathroom door, and when Tom came back followed by a cloud of natural gas. Pity those with a more acute sense of smell or more delicate stomachs. Over the months and years in the community, my own sense of smell had been beaten into a state of permanent numbness, which was no small blessing.

With the luck of the cards I managed to win this second game quite handily, but for Byron it was a kind of victory to avoid being skunked by managing to peg his way across the 60-point halfway line before I counted out. He often said, "I don't mind losing but I hate being skunked." "What about the rubber?" I asked. He must have been very tired, because he looked at the hulk in the doorway and said, "Come on, Tom, you show him how to play." Byron gave up his chair to Tom and started towards the door, but just before leaving, he winked at Mary, who was busily trying to unravel the wool for a scarf she was knitting, and said to her, "Thanks again for the coffee, Sweets." Mary responded with the first line of one of Byron's favourite songs: "How high is the water, Mama?" To which he responded, "Six feet high and risin'." Mary screeched with delight.

The sunroom lost much of its lustre as Byron went off for a rest.

★ ★ ★ ★ ★

MEANWHILE, BACK AT THE RANCH

Dear Mum and Dad,

Last night Mary was telling a story about when she found a bat in our living room, telling it for approximately the 10 billionth time. She was saying that she screamed because if a bat gets in your hair you lose all of it and it never grows back, ever. Then someone asked her why it never grows back and she said, "Oh, they eat the roots right out of your head."

I was starting to laugh and she was getting angry and starting to list all the unquestionable sources of this piece of information and then Byron chipped in, with a totally serious and slightly alarmed and solicitous look on his face.

"No, it's absolutely true. I had this friend and the bat ate the hair roots right out of his head and once it'd finished them it chewed his ears off, too."

————

October 1985

Mary was in a fine mood tonight, because she sold so many pumpkins at the roadside today, and also because Byron is home.

Tonight Mary taught Kevin how to knit, using some cruelly stiff hideous green wool that must have been used for making mats in dog pounds. Kevin was getting worried because it didn't look right and Mary said, "Oh, you have to knit two or three rows before it looks right, it's like a baby, they're abnormal for the first year or two…" Then she looks around happily when we laugh and says, "I really do come out with some good ones sometimes, don't I?"

There is a freedom in being with people who have nothing to lose, who know their own inadequacy without a shadow of doubt. The rest of us waste so much energy trying to kid ourselves we are something more.

Lots of love,
Weesa

8

Christmas Tree Bypass

There was a mountain of pain and anger in Byron that could erupt at the slightest provocation, and when it did there followed a kind of shockwave of anger that he directed against himself. I was rarely the target of his anger, but I always found it so frightening that I invested considerable energy in trying to protect the household and Byron from these volcanic eruptions. Our weekly house meetings were sometimes the occasion for setting Byron off.

At one such meeting, Nadine, a young woman who had recently joined the community through the Jesuit Companions Program, was taking her turn to share how she had lived the past week. She told us that she was feeling the need to take more time to pray, but was finding our chapel not conducive to prayer because of its lack of privacy. She complained that since this room was used as a passageway for Byron and me to go in and out of our room, it did not work as a prayer room. I felt my stomach tightening as she spoke, and I looked at Byron, knowing he was not going to receive this well. A couple of other people concurred with Nadine. I quickly spoke up and suggested that the two of us would try to be more attentive to the presence of people in the chapel, and at such times, we would take the long way around through the living room to get to or from our room. Nadine and others were not satisfied with this solution, saying that we would still have to open the door of the chapel to see if it was occupied and this would already be a distraction to whoever was in there. Byron said nothing but I could see from his pale, drawn face that he was fuming inside. The solution that others seemed to favour was putting a latch on the inside of the doors so that whoever was in there could assure their privacy. It seemed we had come to a consensus in the matter because neither Byron nor I made any strong objection to the plan. I said nothing out of fear that if the discussion continued any longer the volcano would erupt with disastrous consequences. Besides, I had been in the community long enough to know that most of these bright ideas never got put into action. I suspect that Byron could not speak because he was putting all his energy into controlling his rage.

Two days later, when Byron discovered the latches that Kevin had dutifully put on the chapel doors, he tore them off and threw them into the equally raging fire in the wood stove. To my surprise, he did not head straight to town to get drunk. Thanks to Kevin's gentle, persistent manner, the two of them managed to talk through this issue and seemingly come to a peaceful acceptance of each other's position. A couple of hours later, however, Byron did go into town for wine. When he returned to the house he was still sober enough for us to talk.

He told me, with tears in his eyes, how upset he was and that he had been driving around looking for a good tree from which to hang himself. It seemed to comfort him to hear me say how important our friendship was to me, and that I really needed him and so did the community. He continued drinking for several days, which brought up in me a mixture of fear and anger. Sitting alone one night in the chapel I began to cry, which helped me realize that my deepest pain with Byron's drinking was loneliness. When he withdrew into alcohol I dearly missed him. It felt like he had gone away and might never return.

The following Wednesday during our house meeting, we reviewed the decision about the chapel. Byron was there even though he was still drinking a bit. I was very tense during the hour-and-a-half meeting and over-protective of Byron, which must have been frustrating for the others. The resolution we arrived at – that we would avoid using the chapel as a passageway during the evenings when people might want to pray there and that there would be no latches on the door – was a compromise that did not really satisfy anyone. I suppose we all knew that it meant that nothing was going to change.

Why this matter of having to use the long route through the living room to get to and from our room was such a big issue for Byron was not clear to me at the time. Certainly, part of it was the matter of control. He hated giving up control even in a small matter to this young woman who had only been in the house for a couple of months, and who would probably use the chapel occasionally for a few weeks at most before giving up on her prayer project. I think the deeper issue was the fact that this took place in mid-November, when Byron would already be thinking of Christmas, his most difficult time of year.

Christmas was not an easy time for most of us in the community. For me the Christmas tree epitomized the problem. Putting up a Christmas tree would seem like a lovely communal event to bring the household together and fill us with a sense of warmth and goodness, a spirit of family. Indeed, there was something to this, but there were certainly some very different feelings and experiences as well.

In late November and early December I would do some tree spotting as I walked in the extensive bush areas on our farm. When it came time to actually go out and cut down a tree, I already knew where to lead our small tree-cutting party, thus minimizing the frustration of trying to find just the right tree in 150 acres of bush. There was usually someone in this party who had no sense of proportion and would wonder why we couldn't take home that beautiful spruce, for example, that was taller than a three-storey building. Someone else, of course, would insist on a pine, one that would have filled the entire living room if we had been able to get it into the house. I would lead the group to the tree I had already selected, and help them realize that this was *our* best choice. I would often say, and sometimes actually believe, it was the tree that chose us. Byron never showed the slightest interest in getting a tree, and my intuition told me that the less I talked about it in his presence the better. In fact, my pre-selecting the tree probably had something to do with minimizing the matter somehow for Byron's sake, even though he would not even be with us in the bush.

There would be some discussion about when to put up the tree, and I for one always pushed for the latest possible date, not more than two or three days before Christmas. Usually there were one or two young people in the house for whom it was their first Christmas away from home. Their enthusiasm would help get things going with regards to getting the tree up and decorated. Maggie was such a person. She put tremendous energy into trying to make Christmas in the Farm House everything that Christmas back home had been for her, her parents and her numerous siblings. Her mother obviously wore herself ragged for her large family during the festive season, and Maggie was not going to be outdone by Mom. She was up all night for many nights knitting and decorating individualized Christmas stockings for each one of us. Then there was the baking of batches of special cookies with her grandmother's favourite recipes, and on and on it went. So for Maggie the tree decorating, followed, of course, with hot chocolate, marshmallows and cookies, was of paramount importance. It just wouldn't be Christmas without this. We would all participate and we would all enjoy it, just as she and her siblings had always done.

The only hitch in this plan was that we were neither Maggie's siblings nor her children, and our previous experiences of Christmas and Christmas trees were radically different. Well, the tree did get decorated, but it wasn't exactly a perfect moment of family fun. Two or three diehards managed to stay with the project from the moment the decorations were brought out of storage in the basement to the throwing on of the last bits of tinsel. As soon as I made sure that the tree was standing secure in the correct place (always the same corner every year) I would withdraw for a while from the enterprise to visit briefly with Byron out in the sunroom, as far away from the living room as he could get. There we would talk about anything but the rituals of Christmas.

Mary, the Russian Princess, would go at the decorating in her usual determined way, impatient to have the task complete. She would quickly hang a bunch of bright bulbs on the tree, each time asking and getting my approval: "Mary, that's perfect, you are doing great, you sure know how to decorate a tree." In turn I often asked her approval for where I was placing the various decorations, but would not get the same unconditional affirmation: "You've got too many of those blue ones all in the same place; who taught you how to decorate a tree?" She, too, needed to withdraw from time to time and go have a cigarette with Byron.

For some of our people, decorating a Christmas tree was an entirely new experience, not because of their religious background but because of the broken situations in which they had grown up. For Wayne, for example, many ordinary things that we take for granted were totally new. When Christine introduced him to the house and pointed out the sheets for his bed, he said in all innocence, "What are those things?" Once, when Wayne had surprised and delighted me by cleaning up the kitchen without being asked, I said to him, "Wayne, you are a living saint; when you die they're going to canonize you." He responded with panic in his voice: "Oh, no, I want to be buried at sea."

Perhaps the reason Wayne had done this surprising thing of cleaning up the kitchen was something that had happened a couple of months before this. I had arrived home from a weekend away at a time when Christine was no longer in the house. Coming into the kitchen I was shocked to see it in such a mess, with the sink and counters loaded with two days' worth of dirty dishes. Something inside me snapped and I started shouting something about this being a home and not a pigpen, and grabbing handfuls of the unwashed cutlery, including some large metal serving spoons, and flinging them clattering to the floor. Wayne and the others sitting around the table stared with stunned amazement, but probably none of them was as shocked as I was by this uncharacteristic behaviour. I was even more surprised by the sense of release and inner joy that it gave me. I watched with amusement everyone springing into action, like in one of those old slapstick silent movies. More frequent displays of my anger could have been healthy for me and the community.

Wayne managed to get into more than a few conflicts with Byron and others. On one occasion someone stole a pair of Byron's boots. These were a fine pair of cowboy boots that his brother had sent him from Alberta. Byron was livid and used this as one more occasion to get drunk. We were certain that Wayne, who had some ownership issues, was the culprit. I confronted him on the matter but he steadfastly denied having done it. A month later I discovered that it was Fred who had stolen the boots, probably to sell in order to buy laxatives, part of his bulimia behaviour. I had to apologize to Wayne for the false accusation. He complained bitterly, "Nobody trusts me." I tried to explain to him that when someone has been untrustworthy it takes time to regain people's trust, but that it can be done. I told him he could still make something beautiful out of his life, just like a little acorn can grow into a magnificent oak tree. He responded, "Once a tree has been cut down it can only become a bush." I had much to learn from Wayne.

In any case, Wayne and others like him approached the tree-decorating with a mixture of wonder and uncertainty.

When it came to someone like Frank, who was legally blind, there was great resistance to participating. He actually could see well enough to do it, but I suspect some unhappy past experiences had undermined his confidence. Being very near-sighted, Frank could only see things well when they were just beyond the tip of his nose. If he ever dropped and broke a tree ornament he would be doubly embarrassed, thinking that such an accident singled him out as being different and inadequate. Such "failures" remained imbedded in his unrelenting memory. It would be no help to try to convince him that accidents happen just as frequently to those who have good eyesight. I will never forget the day in our farm workshop when Frank was doing one of his usual chores of counting the day's eggs that had been cleaned, weighed and put into cartons. Frank, in his usual slow, methodical way, was counting egg by egg, carton by carton. Thanks to our 200 productive hens there were many cartons of eggs. It was five in the evening, the end of our workday, and I was impatient to get home for supper. Every time I intervened to try and speed up the process Frank would lose his count and begin all over again. Several times he refused my offer of help. Finally, I thought that a little guilt might work so I said, "Frank, when you don't let me help you it makes me feel useless." He came up to me and, with his nose almost touching mine so that he could look into my eyes, said in his loud, clear voice, "I often feel that way." Thus, it was only with considerable coaxing that we managed to get Frank past the fear of failure and the risk of feeling more useless so that he could hang a decoration or two. He was really much more interested in the cookies and hot chocolate with marshmallows that would follow.

To Maggie's great disappointment, there would usually be one or two others, like Byron, who avoided the whole event. One of those years, I had an experience that helped me understand what was going on here.

I had been asked to lead a worship service in a Catholic high school to help the students enter into the experience of Christmas. I was speaking to them about different attitudes we can have during this season, such as hoping to receive a great deal, or on the other hand looking to how we can give of ourselves to make this a good experience for others. At that point an example from my own life popped into my head: I began to tell them of an experience of my own when I was in high school. I started to explain that when it came time to decorate the family Christmas tree, I had found myself doing it all alone. As I said this, to my utter surprise I had to fight back the tears. I was for a moment 14 years old back in the living room of our little house in Oakville, standing in front of the fir tree that Dad and perhaps all of us would have dragged home on a toboggan a few days earlier. The lights were strung on the tree but nothing else as yet. I was holding with both hands a fragile bright red ornament, my favourite, wondering where to begin and trying to muster the courage to begin. I have no recollection of where my parents and siblings were at the time but there I was alone, very much alone. Now, 30 years later, standing before these high school students, I was discovering for the first time the depth of pain that was attached to that event. Even now I wonder how much that buried pain continued to affect subsequent tree trimmings. Most of my conscious memories of Christmas were pleasant, marked with a spirit of joyful excitement. Mom and Dad, in spite of the fact that their financial resources were very limited, always made sure that Santa came with abundant gifts for each one of their children. Christmas dinner never lacked for anything. However, this probably was achieved at great psychic cost to them, which would help to explain why in later years Christmas always seemed to be an especially difficult time for Mom. When she was drinking this would be the season when the problem was most out of control. If she wasn't drinking, this could be the time she would start drinking again.

If decorating a Christmas tree could carry that much pain for someone like me, who for the most part had had a happy childhood, how much more pain could there be for some of our people who came from very broken family situations? For Byron there could have been many painful Christmas experiences, but his greatest suffering now was being cut off from his wife and daughters, whom he missed more at Christmas than at any other time. This was the one blessing of not having a nose; at least he did not have to deal with the painful associations connected with the smells that filled the house: the pungent scent of spruce or pine wafting out of the living room, and the various aromas of things baking in the kitchen. But he could see. He told me that he tried to get through the entire season without even seeing the tree. There would be no way of avoiding this if the chapel door was latched closed and he had to pass through the length of the living room to get to and from our bedroom. Byron may have taken a lot of bypasses in his days of trucking, but this was one bypass he was going to do his best to avoid.

★ ★ ★ ★ ★

MEANWHILE BACK AT THE RANCH

Dear Mum and Dad,

We had hamburgers for supper and everyone took them into the living room to watch the Super Bowl, the Bears against the Patriots. I went in for a while and all I could make out was dozens of people running about and jumping all over each other or up in the air. So I took my hamburger and went into the kitchen, and Mary, our "Russian Princess," came and joined me. She was getting a bit pissed off because everyone was paying attention to the Super Bowl and not to her. She began to do the washing up very noisily, long before the meal was finished. When she had washed and dried all the plates and bowls she started sweeping the kitchen floor, every now and then rushing into the living room, saying, "Wait until you see what the kitchen looks like now."

Meanwhile Byron sauntered in and stood with his back to the fire, taking in the scene as he does, never missing a single thing. He is feeling a little fragile these days. He had a drinking bout last weekend, and now he has an infection in his lungs, which frightens him. Then yesterday he had a terrible fight with Wayne. I was upstairs and I heard shouting downstairs. I went down and Byron was at the end of his tether, having listened to the wrestling on TV all day, and then Wayne's ghettoblaster on the kitchen table once the wrestling was finished. The noise drove him nuts, and he was standing there with his fists clenched over Wayne, who was white as a sheet but refusing to turn it off.

I tried to pry myself between them but they didn't part before Byron had smashed his fist down on Wayne's hand, which was protecting the switch at the On position. Wayne didn't move. He was yellow with fright and shaking, and it must have been painful, but the stubbornness in his face was amazing to see. He sat at the kitchen table pretending to read the newspapers for a good 10 minutes before he retreated to his room. Byron is still feeling a little ashamed. But I can understand that kind of continual noise driving a person to violence. You, Mum, for example, if you were stuck in a doctor's waiting room with elevator music on for a few hours would eventually put a fist through the admissions office window.

Pray for us,
Love from
Weesa

9

Strength in Weakness

In the spring of 1985, the community was at a moment of unprecedented strength. Our two community homes were filled to capacity, including the creation of a new bedroom with a couple of extra beds in the Farm House when we winterized the workshop behind the house. We had purchased a nearby home for Harry and Peg and their six children. By the labour of our own hands and with lumber taken from our woodlot we had completed the construction of a fine new home, which was occupied by the newly arrived assistant farm manager and his wife and four children. It was indeed with some pride and confidence that we as a flourishing community were now able to articulate the statement of our vision:

> Ignatius Farm Community is a Christian Community of healing and growth. It is made up of women, men and children; laity and people with religious vows; single people and families.
>
> It is a community of welcome that does not deny or reject human weakness and need. Rather it believes that our human poverty, our woundedness can be a privileged point of meeting both with God and with one another.

It is a farming community that draws nourishment and healing from the land and strives to be faithful and just in its stewardship of the land.

It is a community committed to justice both within the community itself and in the larger society. In solidarity with other farmers we are committed to the struggle for justice in the areas of agriculture and food.

It is a community that tries to live simply, in solidarity with the oppressed and the poor.

It is a community nourished by the Eucharist and other forms of communal and personal prayer and celebration.

It is an apostolate of Ignatius College.

The way of proceeding in our life together is outlined in the document *Four Levels, One Way: unconditional acceptance, intensive caring, non-punishment, the right to love.*

The way of governing is spiritual government based on love and trust and proceeding by way of discernment and consensus.

To name the importance of weakness and need in the community turned out to be more prophetic than descriptive. From that peak moment the community was suddenly to be plunged into a valley of great fragility.

On the Labour Day weekend of 1985, most of the community took to the road for a holiday time together at the Jesuit Camp Ekon on Lake Joseph in Muskoka. Byron, not being into this kind of group fun, had chosen not to go, and I happily stayed back to keep him company. We had just finished a few games of cribbage when the phone call came: "There's been a bad accident, a collision on Highway 69 near MacTier: Harry [Jonker] and his family and Mardi in the station wagon...some have been taken to Parry Sound Hospital."

The nightmare had begun. I was grateful that Byron was there to help me deal with this shocking news, which he was able to absorb more quickly than I.

"That 69 is a dangerous highway. I've had so many close calls up there," he said. "Poor Harry and Peg…it sounds bad." After a series of phone calls between Fr. Doug at Camp Ekon, someone at the Parry Sound Hospital, the assistant farm manager, Pat, who had stayed back to care for the livestock, and me, I learned that Harry had been very badly injured and that it looked like Mardi, a young woman who had joined us through the Jesuit Companions Program, had a fractured pelvis. The rest of Harry's family had suffered only minor cuts and bruises and been badly shaken up. The small group of us who had remained in Guelph came together to support each other and to pray for Harry and the others. We celebrated the Eucharist with as much urgency and attentiveness as I have ever experienced. A little later, Fr. Doug called to inform us that Harry's condition was extremely critical and he was being airlifted to Sunnybrook Hospital in Toronto.

It was decided that I would go to Sunnybrook, and Pat and Paul would go to Camp Ekon to support the people there. Before long I was on my way down Highway 401, my mind and imagination racing as I drove. What could have happened? Harry was such a good driver! How bad could it be? Would he survive? Of all people to be injured, Harry, who was the strongest and most important person in the community. How would we manage without his farming expertise? How would we manage without his great spirit of life, and his sense of humour? And Peg, and the children, how could they cope without him? He had to pull through this.

"Dear God, don't let Harry die…please take care of him…please take care of all of us," I prayed.

Harry was already in emergency when I arrived and it was not possible to see him; however, the doctor came to tell me that he was on his way to surgery, which would take several hours. There was significant brain damage as well as serious damage to his legs. Although his condition was critical, it looked as though he would survive. I called Fr. Doug to tell him what I knew, and then at about 2 a.m. went to a Jesuit house in downtown Toronto to get some rest. I returned to the hospital about 6:30 a.m. to learn that the surgery had just finished, and at 9:30 I was able to see Harry, at least the bit of him that was not covered in bandages. With his one visible eye he gave a sign of recognizing me and he weakly responded as I squeezed his hand. That would be his last sign of awareness before slipping into a deep coma. Doug, Peg and Weesa arrived in the early afternoon and I was relieved to have them join me in helplessly keeping vigil by this badly broken, unresponsive loved one, a vigil that extended into days and then into weeks.

This once powerful man, who had been very much a leader of the community by reason of his abilities and personality, had suddenly become our most fragile member, claiming the central place in the heart of the community and in the hearts of each one of us as we kept watch with him and his family and prayed constantly for his recovery. It would be weeks before we began to see any signs that Harry was regaining some consciousness, and much longer before we saw him take a few faltering steps on his badly damaged legs. He came home just before Christmas, a very different man than the one who had set out for Camp Ekon with the community on that fateful Labour Day weekend. His farming days were over.

I found Byron to be an anchor of security during that difficult time. He may not have been one to deal well with his own inner pain, but he had a remarkable way of receiving others in their pain. All that he had been through and was continuing to suffer in his own life was shaping him into a man of compassion. When I came home feeling weary and discouraged, I knew that Byron understood without my having to say very much. He would not give me advice or even words of comfort, but would start dealing the cards in order to be quietly attentive to me through the playing of cribbage, which was at times almost like a form of shared prayer. Weesa, who was very close to the Jonker family, lived this time sharing deeply in their pain. She told me that she could always go to Byron knowing that she would be accepted and understood. Rarely did she feel the need to explain much to him; she could just let her tears flow and receive from his listening presence a comforting peace and strength.

That was the most overwhelming fall season we ever lived on the farm. There was so much work to do and we were missing our leader and his tremendous capacity to work and to repair our aging equipment that was constantly breaking down; we were also missing his optimism and humour that could keep us going in the toughest times. The autumn colours were spectacular and the crops were superabundant, but I hardly noticed this in the daunting effort to complete the corn harvest and get it chopped and into our two silos.

One Wednesday morning I was sitting in a room in Ignatius College waiting for the weekly community council meeting to begin. The community members were straggling in from the farm. I was feeling very down, struggling against a tidal wave of fatigue and discouragement and dreading this meeting in which we would be discussing "all the problems" the community was facing. As I closed my eyes for a moment's rest, my imagination kicked in and took me back to the previous evening, as I walked wearily from the barn across the fields to the Farm House. As I redid this walk in my mind, I was given the grace to really see the incredible beauty and fruitfulness of the land: the corn, the apples, the tomatoes, the pumpkins and all the other vegetables, as well as the radiance of the trees with their brilliant display of reds and golds. Suddenly, sitting there in the meeting room, I realized that instead of worrying about not being able to harvest everything, I should be giving thanks for the abundance. I heard the voice of Mother Earth or the voice of God speaking through the earth, saying, "See how abundantly fruitful I am. Do not be afraid; I can and I will look after all of you." It was a kind of visionary experience that moved me to deep gratitude, giving me new energy and hope for the community and for Harry and his family. I opened my eyes and looked at the people gathering around me at the table and, sensing their goodness, I was ready to begin the meeting, eager to continue the struggle with them knowing that we were not alone in it.

Prior to Harry's accident we had initiated conversations leading to farming practices by which we could be more just and caring stewards of the land. We had given up the use of destructive chemical fertilizers and were working towards farming more organically, a process that would continue until the present day, when the farm is at the point of being certified organic. As we began to take better care of the earth, we were discovering how the earth was taking better care of us. It was, we were discovering, not simply a challenge to be good stewards but to be creative partners with the earth and her productivity. Personally, I was growing in a deeper love and appreciation for the land. Often, as I walked home across the fields, I experienced a sense of peace and sometimes healing coming to me from the land and its life: the plants, wildflowers, trees, birds, deer, foxes and the like, along with our own livestock. The farm was nourishing and strengthening far more than just our bodies. It seemed to be comforting us and holding us together as a community.

We were all seeing more clearly how much we needed Mother Earth and each other, and realizing that by working together and by trusting in the power that was sustaining us we would be able to cope. In and with Harry the whole community was wounded and, true to our vision, this woundedness was proving to be a privileged point of meeting with one another and with God.

We were to be further tested when Pat decided that he could not take the pressure of being responsible for managing the farm. Other family pressures had arisen as well, so that on the following Labour Day weekend Pat and his family moved away from the community. The Jonkers would remain for two more years before they, too, decided it was time to move on. It was just too painful for them to be constantly faced with all that had been lost through Harry's accident.

With the loss of these two large and wonderful families, the community was never the same. Not only was it greatly diminished in size, but all the life and joy that children can contribute was gone. However, as years went by, other gifts were given to fill these gaping losses.

For one thing, people were welcomed into the community who were able to contribute the same kind of joy and spontaneity as had the children, although they also brought some unique challenges. I think, for example, of Fred Outhouse. He was sent to us by a minister in the Maritimes who was concerned by the fact that Fred's welcome had worn thin in the various help organizations in that part of the country. The welcome was to eventually wear thin in this part of the country as well, but until that time Fred brought us a lot of life. I'll never forget the description he gave us of the bird he had seen while walking in the fields: "It was a Baltimore oriole with a gorgeous gold crown, its wings were bright red with white along the edges, and it had this great long tail with blue and silver feathers." In response to my suggestion that I thought Baltimore orioles were orange and black, he innocently replied, "There's more than one kind of friggin' Baltimore oriole." In another birdwatching moment we pointed out to him a woodcock, to which he responded in disgust, "Now who would name a bird a wood cock?"

Fred, the youngest child in an enormous family of 26, suffered from a serious eating disorder, and in one way or another we all suffered with him. While everyone was asleep Fred would tiptoe down to the kitchen and proceed to eat his way through whatever happened to be in the refrigerator and pantry, then go to the bathroom and throw it all up. Or he might clear his system with a massive dose of laxatives that he would have shoplifted somewhere. I found that he simplified the issue of grocery shopping. I can remember going through the aisles of the local supermarket, saying over and over again almost every time I reached for a particular item, "No sense buying that, Fred will just gobble it up."

Once while walking in the middle of the road on his way home from downtown late at night he was approached by the police. "What's your name and where are you from?" they asked. They were sure he was putting them on when he responded in all sincerity, "I'm Frederick Anthony Outhouse, from the Farm House."

Fred had experienced considerable misunderstanding and rejection in his life, which made him especially attentive towards Byron and anyone whose wounds and sufferings were more evident than his own. He showed an extraordinary tenderness towards Ruthanne, a friend with cerebral palsy who often came to visit. Ruthanne, in spite of her wheelchair dependency, difficult speech and need of help for dressing, eating and so forth, has a very joyful spirit and a great sense of humour. She and Byron were great friends and both of them delighted in Fred and very kindly humoured him in his excessive care for them.

The depth of Fred's tenderness was only matched by the height of Frank's frankness. Frank, a unique man who joined us sometime later, also liked Ruthanne, but he was never quite sure how to relate to her since he had a great need for clarity. Once, when Ruthanne had just arrived at the house and was wheeled into the kitchen, Frank and I were across the room drying the dishes. Ruthanne greeted us and was saying something to me that was not at all easy to decipher. Frank in his always loud, clear voice said, "I can't understand a word she's saying."

"Well, Frank," I said gently but facetiously, "she's still a good person." Ruthanne almost fell out of her wheelchair laughing at Frank's response: "Even the man who shot the Pope is a good person!"

Where Fred truly excelled was in playing the air guitar. He made us feel that we were right there in the front row of his spectacular rock concert, to the point where we could almost hear the music and the screaming audience. Fred would take time to meticulously tune his invisible guitar, then try a few bars to make sure he could remember the tune, then off he went with his whole body gyrating to the beat of his guitar. Several songs later he would play the finale and then triumphantly throw his guitar into the air, as we watched it soar and waited for it to crash.

Fred was only one of the many who, spared from the normal patterns of socialization, revealed ever-new dimensions of the wonder of being human. He helped to keep us from being weighed down by the inevitable burdens that had to be carried, although he also managed to contribute liberally to our pile of burdens. In fact, we finally came to the point where as a community we had to ask if it was possible for us to hang on to Fred, and whether it was good for us and for Fred to keep trying. We reluctantly concluded that Fred should be asked to leave, since his mounting anger seemed to indicate that he no longer wanted to stay. His only question when I told him our decision was, "But you still love me, don't you?" I was able to respond honestly, "Yes, Fred, I still love you."

As the community became smaller, we obviously needed to work together and support one another more than ever. Eventually, the community council was no longer a small governing group making decisions on behalf of a much larger group. It became possible and more effective to have everyone in the community participate directly in the weekly council meetings. It may have been less efficient this way but it was certainly much more fun, and gave everyone a greater sense of ownership and responsibility.

Someone like Frank may have been more interested in the cookies that were being passed around than in the question of whether or not we could afford to buy a new tractor, but he was gifted with a wonderful curiosity. If he ever had to miss a meeting, he wanted to see the minutes as soon as possible and be filled in on every little detail of what had transpired in his absence. Frank was also a living calendar, reminding us well in advance of upcoming birthdays and other important and not so important events, such as an outing to the zoo that had been put on hold several months earlier, or a meeting to discuss farming issues, or a deep-sea fishing trip. This latter event he would recall every year on my birthday, which happened to be July 20. On that day a number of years earlier he had gone with his dad and some other men on this fishing trip, and one of these men had hooked a big fish but it got away. Somehow this event lodged itself in Frank's remarkable memory and needed to be honoured annually. He also had a gift to touch our hearts by the way he prayed: "For all of us, that we may live the true meaning of Christmas by sharing our bread with the hungry and our lives with the lonely and lost." Then, during a solemn Easter Sunday liturgy, he could make everyone laugh by praying "that the Easter Bunny find his way to us at the Farm House and not get run over by a truck on Highway 6 — honk, honk, squish."

Frank helped us to have a sense of balance, showing us how to take everything seriously but nothing too seriously.

At this point in the life of the Farm Community I was experiencing more deeply the gifts that some of our people had for uniting us and getting us through the difficult times. It was Jean Vanier who had first alerted me to looking for the

Bill & his older brother Gord, 1935

Bill & Gord, 1999

Bill with his parents at the Jesuit Novitiate in Guelph, Ontario, 1957

Bill and his friend Fr. Larry Gillick SJ meet Pope John Paul II at
the Vatican (1984)

A detail from a photograph of the Regis College (Willowdale) Ordination
Class, 1966

The Farm House in Autumn

Fred Outhouse and Weesa (Louisa) Blair forking manure

Byron heading for his bedroom with a little lunch

Byron on Patches and Lorraine Busch on Babes, behind the Farm House

A New Year's Day Mass in the barn. Mary Bastedo from l'Arche Daybreak is playing the guitar to Bill's left.

Byron in his chair

Byron and Bill in the Farm House kitchen holding salmon after a fishing trip to Owen Sound

Bill and Byron playing cribbage in the Farm House

Bill with Jean Vanier at Trosly–Breuil, France, 2003

Byron in his truck

hidden treasure in the people who are often ignored or rejected in our busy, competitive, efficiency-driven societies. Jean was one of the two main speakers at an ecumenical conference for students preparing for ministry that took place in Montreal in 1966. I had the privilege of participating in that conference and was deeply moved by Jean's integrity and the uniqueness of his message. Jean spoke about the people with whom he was sharing life in the l'Arche community he had helped to found two years earlier in France, people who in some ways were the poorest of the poor. He spoke of what he was learning from these people who, because of their limitations and all they suffer from humiliation and rejection, more readily recognize their need for others. Because they live more from their hearts they are especially open to and capable of intimacy with God, who communicates directly to the heart. Their poverty, their vulnerability, helps to disarm us so-called able people and invites us to accept our own poverty and find in our vulnerability this meeting place with God and others. Jean talked a great deal about the importance of community and the way his people were teaching him how to live it. They did not need him as a former naval officer giving orders and organizing their lives. They needed him as a friend who would open his heart to them.

It was not Jean but Raphael, one of the first men welcomed into l'Arche, a man able to mumble only a dozen words or so, who in a matter of weeks had made friends with all the elderly and most of the children in the village. One of the few words Raphael could say was "*marier,*" to marry, and marriage was his constant theme. For him, like all of these "little ones," relationship was what he longed for and what he was constantly calling others into. These people at the heart of l'Arche were always asking, with or without words, the fundamental human question: "Do you love me and will you stay with me?" So while there seems to be no place in our competitive, consumer societies for them, finding their place at the heart of this community they were revealing so much about the longing of every human heart, the uniqueness of every human being. They were revealing to Jean and to all of us who we really are and what can happen between us when we begin to let down our defences and accept our inner poverty and vulnerability – not as a curse, but as a gift and blessing.

Maybe I was especially drawn to Jean's message because of my childhood experiences growing up as a visible minority and as the youngest member in my family, which left me with the inner feeling of always being somewhat marginal and insignificant. In any case, it was an exciting and attractive message that convinced me to go to l'Arche and experience for myself this unusual community. After I was ordained to the priesthood later that year, 1966, and completed one more year of theology studies, I went to Spain for the final year of Jesuit formation, which we call Tertianship. We see this experience as a school of the heart, a time of extended prayer and of reflection on our Jesuit life. During this year I went to l'Arche in Trosly-Breuil, a village about an hour north of Paris, and lived there for a month. This was truly schooling for my heart, which was captured by the deep acceptance and love I received from the people there. At the end of this month I returned to Spain to complete Tertianship but I never really left l'Arche.

After Tertianship I began doctoral studies in Christian spirituality at the *Institut Catholique* in Paris. The longing for community that led me to join the Jesuits had been deepened by my experience of l'Arche, so that when it came time to do my thesis it was at least clear that I should do something on community. I first began reading the letters of the 17th-century French Jesuits and their companions working with the aboriginal people of Huronia in what is now the Midland area of Ontario, a number of whom were martyred by the Iroquois, the long-time enemies of the Hurons. These Jesuits, these "Black

Robes," had to abandon their French culture to enter deeply into the lives and culture of their hosts: the arduous journey by canoe, including many portages, from the settlements in what is now Quebec to the Huron villages on Georgian Bay; sleeping in the smoke-filled, flea-infested longhouses; and eating whatever gruel was dished out of the common cooking pots. While giving their lives for and with the Hurons, they had little to say explicitly about community, even though they were living it in a very radical way. Meanwhile, since I was staying in contact with Jean Vanier and l'Arche, it eventually occurred to me that this revolutionary community, which held the weakest and most vulnerable at its heart, was precisely what I needed to study as my thesis topic.

The Jesuits in Huronia lay down their lives to evangelize "the poor," although in many ways the Hurons, with their own culture and spirituality, were not so poor. In 1969–1971, when I was living in l'Arche, I was discovering its mystery: namely, that it is the poor who do the evangelizing. Those Jesuits knew that the Church was especially for the poor, but l'Arche is revealing that, while indeed the Church is for the poor, more fundamentally, it is the Church that needs the poor. They hold the secret of who Jesus really is and how to open our hearts to his tender and vulnerable heart. The people I came to know and love at l'Arche were helping me come to a deeper knowledge and love of Jesus and of the community he founded first and foremost for the poor. I never completed the thesis, but I did complete *Enough Room for Joy: Jean Vanier's l'Arche, A Message for Our Time* (McClelland and Stewart, 1974), a book that is now out of print but which in its time helped a number of people to discover l'Arche.

The Farm Community, being a Jesuit apostolate, obviously drew even greater direct support from the Jesuits and their charism than did l'Arche. However, it remained much more fragile and chaotic than most of the l'Arche communities I know. Unlike most of these communities, the Farm Community received no direct government support, which also meant that it was not accountable to government. While such accountability can be a support to community, it also limits freedom and flexibility. The Farm Community was free to welcome people who fell through the cracks in the social welfare system because they could not be easily defined and labelled. We were also free to welcome people from any part of the country and even refugee claimants from other countries. There was in the Farm Community no clear distinction between the helpers and the helped, something that would be unthinkable in a social service agency.

We of course constantly failed at living up to our four levels of caring – unconditional acceptance, non-punishment, intensive caring and the right to love – but we kept coming back to these as our reference point. Many of the people we welcomed were deeply wounded by a life filled with the opposite of these four levels. Dan, for example, at a very early age was given up to Children's Aid along with his sister by his single mother, who seemed incapable of caring for them. Eventually, his sister was reclaimed by their mother, but not Dan. He experienced a childhood full of punishment, as he was bounced from group home to group home, about 20 of them in all. Like a critically ill person placed in the intensive care unit of a hospital, Dan and others like him needed intensive care to heal the deep and almost fatal wounds caused by rejection and punishment. This was a challenge. When Dan arrived his insecurity and hurts impelled him to talk incessantly. It is not easy to be attentively present to someone who is constantly talking at you. This was a ministry of presence, just living and working together. We could hang in with Dan more easily than with some because he was not physically violent, he was not threatening anyone. When people were physically violent, threatening to do serious harm to someone or acting out unlawfully, like stealing cars, we had to let them go. But we couldn't get rid of someone for talking too much, no matter how oppressive this could be at times. A year or two of the intensive caring of presence and listening brought some peace to Dan so that he didn't need to talk quite so much. After two years with us he announced that this was the longest time he had ever lived in one place, and that this was going to be his home for life. Dan did remain until the community had to close. He learned to handle the tractors and some of the farm machinery and was a big help to the farm manager. Of course, he was a challenge as well, as he sometimes thought he knew best how to manage the farm, and listening was not his best gift. Dan was one of the most welcoming people we had. He was offered and claimed the right to love. Dan had a wonderful way with people, especially with children, and no one was better at telling people all about the community and giving them an exhaustive detailed tour of the farm. His past hurts meant that he continued to be more attentive to the negative aspect of things but that was understandable. When visitors were shown the newborn calves they would probably hear much more about the two that died than the 42 healthy ones they could see frolicking in the field. Even the most intensive caring can't heal all wounds, and there are always scars that remain.

Our way of operating was a striking alternative to the social agency model. The Jesuit Brother Jim McSheffrey arrived in the community with a degree in social work and fresh from the experience of working in an agency. He found the adjustment very difficult. Jim was kind and generous to a fault but he could not readily agree with the Farm Community policy of unconditional acceptance and non-punishment. He shared a room in the Red House with Wayne, who at that time had some serious hygiene problems, a habit of taking things that didn't belong to him, and refused or was simply unable to keep his side of the room in order. Jim wanted to give him an ultimatum: change or else. Sharing a room with Wayne at that time would have been no joke, so no one could blame Jim for wanting to see him shape up, but Doug and the community council could not support the idea of ultimatums and sanctions. That was just not our way of proceeding. We believed that people needed to be encouraged to change, supported, and at times challenged, but we were against trying to force change. Wayne did gradually make significant progress in the development of social skills, but Jim stayed only three years in the community, which was hardly long enough to witness this progress. Wayne, Byron and many others would not have survived long if the community had operated on good social work principles.

Jim, on the other hand, had to be accepted and respected in the community for who he was. Fortunately, his own inner goodness was stronger than his social work principles, so he was able to live well there in spite of the frustration he experienced. It was that goodness that really shone through in his later life and work with the disadvantaged people of the Mount Scio or MacMorran community in St John's, Newfoundland. There he was able to be more his own person and give himself completely in the service of others out of a deep sense of social justice that went beyond any social agency model. The great work he was doing in St. John's came to an all too sudden end with his tragic death. He was picking berries at the time, something he dearly loved to do, but his drive always to do more and his klutziness put him in mortal danger reaching for the best berries hanging over a cliff several hundred feet above the ocean. (We in the Farm Community knew about Jim's way of working. When he would go into the bush to cut trees with the chainsaw he and anyone working with him were at risk. Harry used to say, "Even our more suicidal members are afraid to go into the bush with McSheffrey.") It was several days before Jim's body was found washed up on the shore. He was and continues to be deeply mourned by the thousands of people whose lives he touched. In her book *A Faith that*

Challenges (Novalis, 2002), written in tribute and gratitude for Jim, Maura Hanrahan writes:

> I was chewed up with grief for this humble, unassuming man who saw Jesus, his saviour, in absolutely everyone. I could see now how well he had lived this simple, powerful theology; I felt profoundly touched by this. And I knew that hundreds of other people felt as desperately sad as I did, all across the mourning city and far beyond.

The Farm Community's way of proceeding and its lack of clarity was, however, a weakness as well as a strength. For one thing, with roles and responsibilities not clearly defined, either a few people would end up doing too much or things simply didn't get done at all because no one took responsibility. Also, it was difficult to find ways to support those who in fact were carrying greater responsibility, or to call to accountability those who were avoiding it. There were many needs that went unmet.

I became especially aware of how true this was when my friend Margo came for a visit, her first and last. Margo, a wonderfully generous and caring woman and a very close friend of Jean Vanier's mother, had raised her family of three daughters and cared tenderly for her husband through his extended terminal illness. She came to spend a week at the Farm House with the intention of being of help to us. The immensity of the needs that she immediately perceived was all but overwhelming: need for greater order and cleanliness in the house but especially the deep needs of people that tore at her motherly heart. Through her eyes I also began to see some of these needs more clearly, which was a bit frightening for me. The morning after her arrival she came to me and asked, "Where do I begin?" Realizing that she would quickly exhaust herself without making the slightest inroads into the chaos, I took her by the arm, led her into our little chapel and said, "You can start here." It was clear to me that this woman of prayer could offer the greatest help by interceding for us before the God of Mercy.

Margo stayed only a couple of days, but I know she carried us home in her heart and kept on pleading to God on our behalf.

There were some distinctions that the community could not deny. For example, those on disability pensions paid room and board while others did not. Everyone received a weekly stipend of $30 no matter how hard or how little they worked. Some, because of the added responsibility they were carrying, needed and got at least one day off during the workweek. Others would have been lost with too much time on their hands. Because the differences were not clearly named and articulated, they were at times sources of resentment and conflict. In spite of these difficulties, we valued the fact that people did not need to be labelled and that everyone could share in the responsibilities according to their particular strengths and weaknesses. Harry's accident, therefore, did not change his status. Although he could no longer work on the farm, he continued to be a treasured member of the community.

Now, following the accident, in this our time of greatest need, it was becoming more evident that it wasn't our strengths or hard work and good organization that were holding the community together, and it was not Doug's or my leadership gifts, nor was it the Jesuit charism. All of these were a help, but key to our survival were the people with their wounds and weaknesses and even their addictions and compulsions. Byron, Fred, Frank and Harry after his accident, those who could not easily hide their wounds, were reminding all of us that we are wounded, but they were also revealing to us how these wounds could be the source of life and even of healing for one another. They were the ones who because of their wounds were most deeply living the first beatitude of the Gospel of Jesus, "Blessed are you who are poor, for the reign of God is yours" (Luke 6:20). They were the ones keeping the community rooted in the reign of God, reminding all of us as individuals and as a group that on our own we could do very little. We needed others and we needed God.

This was a community very different from the traditional, structured form lived in most religious congregations of priests, brothers or sisters. These would often be more institutional in style, sometimes linked to a parish, high school, college or other such institution. As a Jesuit I was formed to become capable of functioning independently, to become a strong, self-possessed individual. This "formation" did not come from the depth of our spirituality but rather from the prevailing religious culture in which we lived. In this culture we understood that weaknesses were to be overcome rather than embraced as an important meeting place with God and others. The weaker, less competent members tend to be bypassed or in some way marginalized, or at least certainly not seen as the most precious members to be held at the heart of community. Furthermore, religious communities are structured on the basis of canon law and elaborate constitutions, which structures tend to minimize the importance of individual personalities with their unique strengths and weaknesses. Like many Jesuits, I am very capable of hiding and at times denying weaknesses, and have considerable difficulty sharing them with my confreres. Sometimes our strengths and gifts can even lead us to compete with each other. However, in recent years as we face the crisis of diminishing numbers and questions of relevance and even survival, this tendency towards rugged individualism and self-sufficiency is giving way to a humbler stance towards one another and towards the rest of the world. Furthermore, the last three General Congregations of the Jesuits, beginning with the 32nd held in 1974–75, have invited us to acknowledge that to be a Jesuit is to be a sinner, albeit a sinner loved by Jesus and called into companionship with him. We are challenged in our mission of spreading the faith to see that an integral part of this mission is the struggle for justice in our world. We are called to have a preferential option for the victims of injustice, the poor. We now recognize in a deeper way our need for the poor: the poor within us, the poor among us, and the poor around us. It was in the light of this deepening Jesuit awareness that the Farm Community came into being.

As different as most Jesuit communities may be from l'Arche, Ignatius Farm Community as an expression of the Jesuits' fundamental option for the poor integrates these two prophetic missions in the Church. In his book *An Ark for the Poor* (Novalis, 1995), Jean Vanier pointed out how Jesuit spirituality has complementary gifts that are very important to l'Arche communities: "The Jesuits have a particular charism for giving individual retreats and accompanying people in their spiritual journey. Many [l'Arche] communities and assistants have been deeply nourished, sustained, enlightened, guided and affirmed by Jesuit priests." I mentioned in the first chapter the fact that, at an international meeting of l'Arche that took place in Rome, the General Superior of the Jesuits, Fr. Kolvenbach, stated, "L'Arche is a grace to us Jesuits and we can be a grace to l'Arche." It has been a blessed struggle for me in the Farm Community to integrate the spirituality of the Jesuits, with its emphasis on following Jesus in the service of others, and that of l'Arche, with its emphasis on covenant relationships with Jesus and with his beloved "little ones" who epitomize the spirit of the beatitudes. Both of these spiritual traditions are fundamentally important places of nourishment and belonging for me.

Living in the mess of the Farm Community with Byron and the others was more painful than anything I had previously experienced in Jesuit communities, but it was also more joyful, putting me and keeping me more in touch with my feelings, with my heart. It helped me to be more deeply rooted in the Jesuits and in our spirituality.

* * * * *

MEANWHILE, BACK AT THE RANCH

March 16, 1985

Dear Mum and Dad,

It's the evening after a wild Saint Patrick's Day party. Fred is sitting at the table talking a blue streak. He never ever stops. I wore a plastic netting curtain to the party because it was the only green thing I could find. It was great fun, apart from a moment of tension when Fred started hyperventilating himself with a balloon (a green one).

Fred is the latest addition to our house and I hope the last. We are 10 now and have no more room. He's spent most of his life in institutions and then in hostels in New Brunswick, but no one wants him, not the hospitals or the prisons or the hostels. They all throw him out. He is one of 26 children; I think perhaps he was the straw that broke the camel's back.

When he first arrived he freaked me out so much I got ill. I just couldn't see how we were going to handle him. He is hyperactive and anorexic and bulimic. His eating habits are completely out of control: he starves himself and then stuffs himself and then makes himself sick, sometimes violently, sometimes for half an hour at a time. There is no soundproofing in the house. He also evacuates the food by overdoses on laxatives, which he shoplifts. He eats everything in the house. If there's nothing left in the fridge he goes into the pantry and stirs up flour and sugar in a bowl and eats it. We come down in the morning and the cupboard is literally bare, and most of its contents already down the toilet. I get so furious I could hit

139

him. All our hard work going through his body and directly into the sewers.

But somehow we are coping, and he is calming down a bit. He's an incredible actor, and tells wild exaggerated stories, egged on gleefully by Byron, acting it all out with extraordinary facial contortions. He is like a child, somehow innocent. We had a birthday party for him today, with presents and a cake. He was so happy. He had never had such a birthday.

––––

Late September 1985

Right now I'm sitting in the kitchen at 9:50 p.m. I've hardly had five minutes even to sit and digest all that's going on, not even to sit and digest what's going into my stomach, when I'm not too tired to eat. When I finally staggered into the house tonight we had two wagonloads of straw waiting to be unloaded in the barn, two huge piles of grain waiting to be loaded into the bins and another wagon of silage waiting to be loaded into the silo. On top of that we have the garden bursting with vegetables to be processed or sold at the market, and we have 25 cows on the point of delivery, and new cows being born every day and night, which means we have to get up and check them at 11 p.m. and 3 a.m. This weekend Paul and Halinka are getting married, and we are providing a lot of the food. I have been making a massive potato salad for the past three hours or so.

I am coming to realize that this is how most farmers live. Pat O'Connor says this isn't nearly as tense as when he was farming alone. He says in those days he'd get a twitch in his cheeks and he couldn't sleep at night for the tension. I could really understand farmers taking to alcohol or being violent with their children.

Harry is still in a coma. They operated again on him today to get the water off his brain. In addition to what is happening on the farm we also have to try and get Peg into Toronto every day to see Harry, and have the children to supper, and babysit them at their house until she comes home at night.

I don't know how I keep going but somehow I do. God doesn't seem to be letting us go under, he keeps giving us the strength to go on. It must be God because I can't see any other way that we could. We have been strengthened and unified by Harry's accident, but it's going to be a long haul.

One very huge blessing is that Fred is away for two weeks at l'Arche in Toronto. I keep praying that they won't send him home early. Byron says he keeps praying that Fred falls down and breaks his neck.

Byron's latest song is:

"And the funniest thing of all

Was two roosters playing ball

The night I stole ole Sammy Morgan's gin."

He is so wonderful. He is always here, welcoming and loving and funny.

Lots of love,

Weesa

10

I Might Have Left My Nose Back There

In early February, because of another bout of recurring bronchitis, Byron had a chest x-ray that revealed a spot on his lungs. I visited him several times during the three days he was hospitalized for a biopsy and other tests. "It looks like those damn cigarettes are going to do me in," he said during my last visit, shaking his head, already convinced of what the biopsy would reveal. Early that evening he phoned me to say, "The doc just gave me the news I didn't want to hear – it's the big C. He says they can operate and take out the tumour. I should get them to cut my hands off while they're at it so I can't smoke anymore."

This call confirmed my worst fears as well, but I tried to sound hopeful as I said, "I'm really sorry to hear this, Pal, but don't worry, we'll get through it. You know that there's always been someone watching over you and they won't let you down now. I'll be in to see you tomorrow afternoon. Is there anything you need?"

"I don't suppose you could bring me a bottle, could you?"

"No, I don't suppose I could, Pal, but maybe some more ginger ale, and I'll bring the crib board and give you another lesson in how to play the game."

"Look, Clarke, I've taught you everything I know about that game, and you still don't know a damn thing. See you tomorrow, Pal. If you can't bring a bottle, how about a gun?"

"Byron, try not to worry, we'll get through it. See you tomorrow, Pal."

A few days later he was home with almost a month to wait until his surgery. Patience was not Byron's strong suit so that was a very, very long month. I did my best to spend more time with him during this period, which was perhaps as much for me as for him. We were both getting more nervous as the date for the surgery approached. The evening before he went to the hospital Byron and I, joined by Weesa, Paul and others who came and went, played cribbage until neither he nor I could keep our eyes open any longer. The next morning the hospital called to say his admittance was postponed a day for lack of a bed. Byron did not hide his displeasure at this news. I spent the rest of the day with him, fearful that he would take to the bottle.

The next day he was admitted to St. Joseph's Hospital. He was more peaceful than he had been in the previous days, resigned to whatever the outcome would be. During the past couple of weeks he had talked about dying, seemingly without any great fear. His greater worry was the possibility of having to live with an extended illness. "If they can't get it all, I'd just as soon die right there on the table than be some kind of a basket case for others to look after and feel sorry for."

He also mused about the possibility of his funeral, noting that he hadn't bothered to put money aside for this. "I've never known them to leave anybody above ground – sooner or later they all seem to get buried."

I was doing my best not to show my own fear, or even acknowledge it to myself. So during that time in the hospital waiting for the surgery we did more reminiscing about the past than discussing the future. Finally, grasping his hand as they began wheeling him down the hall, I told him, "Byron, you are going to come through this just fine, you have to because I can't even think about trying to live without you. God bless you, Pal. I'll see you in a few hours."

Sr. Christine and a friend were already with Byron when I arrived in intensive care that evening. The surgery had gone well. A good part of the right lobe of his lungs had been removed and the surgeon was confident that he had gotten all the cancer. Byron was of course very groggy and all wired up to monitors and intravenous drips but it was a relief just to see him.

His recovery was slow but steady. For his birthday a week later we sent him 13 red roses – one dozen roses and one for the jack. That evening, Christine, Weesa, Paul, Mary the Russian Princess and I went to the hospital to celebrate his birthday. His brother John and John's wife were also there. Byron was pleased that we were able to celebrate mass at his bedside, but he needed help to blow out the single candle on his cake.

The surgery forced some changes in Byron's lifestyle. It did not make him stop smoking, but it made him feel guiltier about doing it, at least for the first little while. It did not change his pattern of drinking, since it seemed he couldn't stop that either. What did change was the work he did. His farm work had already been greatly reduced because of the chronic bronchitis, but now it ceased altogether. He began doing more driving to help Christine, who had moved into Guelph to work with street people. She had begun by opening the Welcome In drop-in centre, and subsequently an emergency shelter and several other places of welcome for the homeless. Byron would do a regular pickup of unsold bread and produce from various stores and make deliveries to the drop-in centre, the food bank and other places of need, including the Farm Community. He would also drive the St. Vincent de Paul truck for members of Christine's team who would be picking up and delivering used furniture.

This work put him more in touch with many of the people living on the fringe of society. These people both amused him and drove him crazy but also called forth his compassion. One day, for example, he had a couple of guys in the truck for the furniture delivery. As Byron was backing up a driveway the fellow leaned in front of the mirror on the passenger side, blocking Byron's vision, and said to this proud and seasoned trucker, "It's okay on my side." Byron may have spoken sharply to him but at least he didn't throttle him. For the most part, he was amazingly patient and compassionate with the people he worked with and worked for. Christine relied on him a great deal since he was extremely responsible and generous to a fault – when he wasn't drinking. He also spent more time at home in the Farm House, becoming something like the official greeter for friends or strangers who might show up during the day looking for me or some other member of the household or canvassing for one thing or another. They were often led down the garden path by Byron's mischievous sense of humour, not knowing where to look for me when told I was "up tarrin' the roof" or "in the back forty shooting groundhogs" (something I might actually be doing if we were together). They could, if they were strangers, be totally shocked just to see him sitting there without a nose.

I may have seen in that face the nobility of an ancient Greek statue, but even when he was wearing his glasses and nose people couldn't help staring at him. In the early days Byron would more commonly respond with anger, glaring viciously at anyone he caught staring. As the years went by he came to be more at peace with himself and his appearance. Sometimes he would amuse himself and shock the staring person by taking hold of his glasses and wiggling his nose up and down a few times.

Once a magician came to perform for the community, delighting us by pulling scarves out of his and other people's ears and rabbits out of hats. Byron, sitting at the back of the room, was enjoying the show along with everyone else. As the magician came to the end of his performance, Byron caught his eye and asked him, "Can you do this one?" Then he quickly lifted his glasses and nose up and down. It was the magician's turn to be amazed, as he demanded from Byron, "How did you do that?" To which Byron gave one of his evasive responses: "Does Eaton's tell Simpson's all *its* business?"

Byron may have been encouraged by a story I once told about my own mother. My mother had that condition whereby the pigmentation went out of her skin, resulting in her brown skin becoming marred with dark and light blotches. Had this experience taken place years earlier, in the '40s or '50s, we might have had some strong feelings about Mom losing her rich, brown colour to become a "white" woman. But now racial issues no longer carry the same weight in Canada, at least not for our family. "Mixed" marriages for my brothers and especially for their children have been celebrated with grace and ease to the point where we are simply one happy family with a continuum of colour tones. One day I was visiting Mom in her little apartment. By this time she had somehow prayed herself into sobriety and was living with deep peace that made it a joy and a blessing to spend time with her. I like to think that maybe my own constant prayer was also a contributing factor towards Mom's liberation from alcohol dependency. During this visit I asked if her skin condition was an embarrassment and a suffering for her.

"I used to feel very badly about it," she told me, and then went on to explain. "I have to walk past this grade school to get to the grocery store. The children often make fun of me, saying, 'There goes the lady with the dirty face.' One day I was sitting here in my apartment feeling very sorry for myself, and I started to think about all the people in hospitals and nursing homes who are so ill or crippled that they can never even get out of their beds. Then I cried, and I asked God to forgive me. I can't feel sorry for myself anymore." Whether or not this story actually influenced Byron I'll never know, but I do know that there was a lovely bond of mutual respect between the two of them.

A difficulty for Byron as he became more accepting of his condition was that he would sometimes just forget to put on his glasses. This was easy to do since he had no problem with his eyesight, the glasses being simply the necessary hanger for his plastic nose. One day he went to the bank, and the moment he stepped in the door he knew something was wrong. People were staring at him in a way that made him feel he had a mask on his face and a gun in his hand. He was tempted to say, "Everybody on the floor," but quickly realized what was amiss and did an about-face to go home for his nose. Once back home Byron was a master at turning these painful situations into funny stories and in no time would have everyone howling with laughter.

There was another famous and much-recounted nose incident on a return trip from the Parry Sound area. He had gone there with Christine and her friend Barbara just to get away for a couple of days. They had left the motel an hour earlier and were well on their way down Highway 69 when Byron realized he wasn't wearing his glasses.

"I might have left my nose back there," he announced. Christine pulled onto the shoulder while Byron, behind her in the back seat, checked to see if it was in his bag. A few moments later an OPP officer pulled off behind them and came up to ask, "You folks having trouble?" Byron stuck his head out the window and said in a desperate voice, "Officer, I've lost my nose." Without a word the officer turned smartly around, got back into his car, and drove away.

After his surgery, Byron seemed to be even more at ease about being seen in the house without his nose. If visitors were shocked to see him like that, as far as he was concerned that was their problem. Friends who came looking for me were always touched by the ease and warmth with which he welcomed them, without any embarrassment for his appearance or the way he would be drooling onto a towel in his lap or the napkins on the front edge of his chair cushion. A couple of women friends especially were always appreciative of the way he would so spontaneously rise and give them a welcoming hug.

These various changes in his lifestyle and growing ease with himself and others were gradual. When he first came home from the hospital he was very weak and discouraged. Almost as soon as he felt strong enough to be up and about he took off to the motel for a two-day drunk. This raised in me that terrible mixture of anger, fear, discouragement and loneliness which, as always, was more bearable once I went to see him. It was only when I started talking about the two of us going away for a week in the sun that he began to perk up.

Paul, a professional engineer who had taken a year's leave of absence from his firm in order to spend the time with us, suggested that we might be able to use his parents' condo in Acapulco.

Paul had been with us for a number of months. He had arrived on the heels of a woman named Cathy from south of the border, whom we affectionately remembered as "Cathy the American." For the three months that she was with us she was constantly comparing things she observed and the manner we did certain things with the way things were in the US. "We don't still have this in the States; we never do that in the States." For her everything here in Canada was second best. Cathy was, of course, a gift to us but we had squeezed her into an already over-crowded house, and all breathed a sigh of relief when she left.

At that point everyone agreed that eleven people were just too many for the house – all but me, that is. I could not totally agree since I, without any consultation with the community, had made a commitment to Paul, who had already confirmed a leave of absence from his company. I managed to persuade the household to at least give Paul a one-month trial period. We did not even have a place for him to sleep, but had to take the extra bed out of Weesa's room and put it in the end of the upstairs hallway for him. We joked that Paul had the longest room in the house, with its own three-piece bathroom at the far end, the only problem being that he had to share it with everyone else in the house. Paul got along so well with everybody in the house and had such a great community spirit that it seemed as though we suddenly had one less person rather than one more, and we were all very sad when it came time for him to leave 10 months later. Each person may have filled more or less the same amount of physical space in the community – one bed, one chair at the dinner table, and so forth – but each person needed and filled a very different amount of psychic space.

Within two weeks we managed to get the okay from Paul's parents, the approval of Byron's doctor, his birth certificate from New Brunswick, and our plane tickets. Then, like two excited schoolboys, we were on our way to Mexico. I could not leave, however, without being very aware of how my absence could affect the community, which was still struggling to cope with the aftermath of the terrible accident that had left Harry our farm manager and consequently the whole community in a state of great fragility.

* * * * *

MEANWHILE, BACK AT THE RANCH

Dear Mum and Dad,

Harry still can't speak yet but he understands you and nods and looks you right in the eye and out of his eyes love just pours. I tell him everything that is happening on the farm and he drinks it all in with rapt attention, and I tell him about his children, or I just sit and look at him and hold his hand, and sometimes he puts his arms around me and kisses me. The other night six of us came up to Sunnybrook Hospital and Doug said mass. Harry followed everything, read all the readings, turned the page in the right place, mouthed all the songs and prayers and responses, ate the bread and drank the wine. It was so moving that I had a hard time not crying my head off. It makes all the struggle and pain and prayers make sense, to see how God's healing is bringing him through. It seems he has just come back from God and is emanating love and approval. It is like visiting a holy man.

Back home Fred has been getting incredibly abusive, cursing and shouting at people every evening. Since Bill is the only one he fears enough to be respectful, and he's away, we've been coping with these violent outbursts every evening. What he needs is 24-hour constant attention and unless he gets it he demands it and achieves it by this incredibly negative behaviour. He simply can't believe that anyone could like him so he makes sure no one ever does. I don't know what can help him but I don't think we can, so in a way this is our failure.

He has gone to live in a hotel for a few days, and we didn't stop him. I refuse to feel guilty and instead am rejoicing in having some peace in the house again, having some food to eat: i.e., something to put on your toast in the morning, something in the cupboard when you go to cook a meal. We can even start baking again. Once he had got through everything in the fridge he would start on the pantry and just eat everything up – everything. Bags of flour, sugar, boxes of cereal. Then he would noisily barf it all up every night. Or shit it out, if he'd managed to shoplift some laxatives from the Big V. One time I caught him coming out of the bathroom at night and I lost my temper at him. I had spent all day labouring on the farm to produce our food and he was barfing it all up. He just looked at me sheepishly and slunk away.

He won't be out of our lives for long; he'll be kicked out of the hotel in no time. Perhaps by the time he comes back I will have summoned up some compassion again.

Love from
Weesa

11

Come Big or Stay Home

The gift of our trip to Acapulco was not so much what we did there but just the fact and the fun of spending this week away together.

Byron's biggest concern about flying was whether we could be in the smoking section of the plane. Once this was assured he could relax, ready to enjoy the trip. If our present non-smoking regulations had been in force at that time Byron would not have made the trip. On the flight down we had the company of a gang of Maritimers, sales people with some large enterprise that was hosting a conference in Puerto Vallarta. They were an increasingly happy bunch of men and a few women who, during the course of the four-hour flight, drank the plane dry. Shaking his head with feigned disgust at the way they were carrying on, Byron thoroughly enjoyed being surrounded by these jovial countrymen even though he was not drinking with them. The party atmosphere made it easier for him to drink his coffees without worrying about how he looked pouring them into his upturned mouth and catching most of the spillage in a bunch of serviettes. He was pleased to discover that, although it was very awkward, he could manage to eat something without lying on his back. So he didn't have to make the whole trip on an empty stomach. After we had deposited the drinking party at Puerto Vallarta, the half-empty plane was suddenly very quiet and Byron fell fast asleep, snoring loudly to prove it.

Our 11th-floor condo turned out to be very comfortable, with a balcony overlooking the ocean that caught the sun from late morning until early evening, a great place to play cribbage, to soak in the sun and just to admire the view, all of which we did to excess with great delight. On the evening of our arrival I was too tired or too lazy to go shopping for food, so I found a can of beans in the pantry and a loaf of bread in the freezer.

"We fly here to this luxury condominium on the ocean and here we are eating like a couple of hobos," chuckled Byron. This was a violation of one of his basic principles, or at least one of his favourite sayings: *Come big or stay home.* The next day we located the Super Super supermarket where we headed directly for the fish department, since Paul's mother had recommended the red snapper as an excellent staple since it was both tasty and easily prepared. My Spanish was a bit rusty but I managed to point out a medium-size fish to the butcher and agreed to have him fillet it for us. It was like a graceful oriental dance the way he sharpened his huge knife and with a few deft strokes produced two perfect fillets.

Then he asked me what I wanted him to do with the remainder of the fish. When I told him the fillets were all we wanted he gave me a funny stare then looked at all the red snapper fillets already on display and then looked back at me and shrugged his huge shoulders. I got the point and said in English, with an embarrassed smile, "I guess it would have been simpler and cheaper to buy them that way, right?" He nodded his assent with a broad smile. But we had our red snapper, and would be back several times for more.

The following day we discovered the huge open market. There were all kinds of fish and meat there, along with acres of fresh produce, as well as clothing and innumerable other goods. When we saw the clouds of flies that swarmed over and around the fish and meat we decided that the market was a great place for people-watching but we would continue to do our shopping with the wealthy Mexicans and tourists in the sparkling clean air-conditioned Super Super – hang the expense. With Byron recovering from major surgery, that was one risk we were happy to avoid. We did return a few times to the open market since we found the people there so fascinating but we never got up the nerve to purchase anything to eat.

One of the views from our balcony was the swimming pool of the adjacent hotel. We did our best not to be voyeurs, but it was hard not to notice and be amused by some of the sunbathers and their outfits, each one a little skimpier than the next – the outfits, that is. "Who am I to be laughing at anybody?" Byron suddenly concluded. "It's just a good thing nobody can see me sitting here in the sun." It is true that he presented a unique picture sitting there in his bright red bathing suit with that magnificent nose-less face of his, and the front of his body getting to be almost as red as the bathing trunks, except for a wide swath of skin angling down across his chest and abdomen that remained a bluish white, almost matching the colour of his thinning, long stringy hair. This swath of skin resistant to tanning or burning was the area from which grafts had been taken for the reconstruction of his jaw, surgery that had eliminated his belly button. He told me with great amusement about a later hospitalization when a nurse's aid was shaving his chest and abdomen in preparation for surgery. She intended to shave him just down to his belly button, and so kept going lower and lower and lower, as he watched her eyes opening wider and wider and wider.

At this time Byron still needed to sleep a great deal, which gave me space to read and to take long walks on the beach. These times of walking in solitude enabled me to reflect on what was being received during these days together. The more painful aspects of our relationship seemed to fade in the light of the gift of our friendship. I was aware that the bond between us was now so deep that it was becoming increasingly difficult for both of us when I had to make extended trips to visit l'Arche communities in other parts of the world and to preach retreats for members of this international federation of communities. I gave thanks for our friendship but wondered about how mutually dependent we were becoming, and to what extent it could be excluding other members of our community. Particular friendships had been discouraged during my early formation as a Jesuit, not without some wisdom, perhaps. Even in families when parents have obvious favourites among their children it can be very hurtful for the others. The Farm Community was not a Jesuit formation house and was not exactly a family, but surely in this matter the same principles would apply. My own ideal of community, that each member should be treated with utmost respect and no one should be ignored, was also at risk here. However, even in the light of all this, I still sensed that at this point I just had to continue welcoming the friendship, and trust that what was gift to the two of us would somehow also be a gift to the community and to others. Certainly, greater freedom in our relationship was needed, but this was a process that would take time and effort as well as a great deal of prayer. The real issue was more a matter of how I could offer similar respect and friendship to others in the community. This, I felt, was no small challenge and maybe even an impossible ideal, but at least something worth struggling for. I was encouraged by remembering a statement of Jean Vanier's: "People who love community can destroy community, but people who love people build community." I prayed for the grace to be more free and selfless in my love for Byron and for each member of the community, knowing that I had a long way to go.

The week went all too quickly, and before we knew it we were back in the Acapulco airport, first in line to be sure we would be in the smoking section for the return flight to Canada. In Puerto Vallarta we picked up the same gang of Maritimers now on their way home. Judging from the smattering of conversations we overheard it had not been a very serious conference. After a couple of hours into the flight they were partied out, with many of them sleeping peacefully. By that time Byron and I had played several hands of crib. We were both very content with our time together and it seemed obvious that it should not be the last of such expeditions. Before we landed I turned to him and said, "Byron, when we get home we have to apply for your passport, so that you can come with me in the fall on my trip to France and Spain." His response was immediate:"I'd love that." So before we were on the ground we were looking forward to our next flight.

Paul and Mary the Russian Princess picked us up at the airport and drove us back to Guelph. They informed us that Julie was going to have to leave for prison tomorrow – sad news that made it difficult to speak with much enthusiasm about our trip. Julie, a lovely and essentially innocent young woman, had been welcomed into the community over a year ago while she awaited trial for killing her baby. It was clear, at that time, that what she needed was a safe, supportive environment where she could be loved into new life. When Christine went to pick her up to bring her to the community, Julie was in leg irons. The magistrate and police were grateful to us for taking her in. During the trial it came out how she had been used by her husband and his girlfriend. They would leave her to babysit the girlfriend's three children as well as look after her own baby. She had to do all the housekeeping, including the piles of dirty dishes they would leave in the sink after their parties, and Julie was a clean freak who could leave nothing undone. After watching a TV soap opera in which a woman stabbed her own baby, Julie did exactly that. When it came to the trial, her lawyer was afraid to put her on the stand for fear she might incriminate herself, but Fr. Doug insisted, saying that once people heard her speak they would realize that her simplicity and lack of any malice absolved her of serious culpability. Julie was the one who, when asked by Weesa if she needed to use the washroom before setting out on a long trip, said, "No, I'll be all right, I have very good lungs." Then there was the Saturday morning she came into the Farm House and was boasting to Byron about how she had done all the chores on her own. Byron remarked that it must have taken her a long time to do all the eggs by herself. In all seriousness she replied, "Oh, no, the chickens don't lay on the weekends."

In the courtroom, when the judge asked Julie if she knew why she was on trial she was able to say, "Yes, manslaughter," but it seemed doubtful if she really knew the meaning of such a big word which she could barely pronounce. She went on to tell the judge of all that she was doing on the farm. When the judge heard this young girl (she was 22 but looked about 15) with her speech impediment boasting about driving the combine harvester, repairing the tractors and so forth, he got the picture.

Given the fact that she was living in the Farm Community she was at first spared from having to do any time in prison. However, concerned about public reaction, the crown had appealed the decision, and now Julie was sentenced to six months, which would begin the following day at the Vanier Correctional Centre for Women.

That evening we all gathered at the Red House, Julie's home, for a vigil of prayer to express support for her and to wish her well. This was a sad moment but one of deep peace and communion as we all did our best to encircle Julie with love and care. Some quiet hymns were sung and we prayed for her and told her our appreciation.

"Julie, you have been a gift to me, your smile, your gentleness have given me a lot of joy"…"Julie, I like you and I will miss you, and I will pray for you every day"…"Julie, I pray that the time will go quickly for you and for us, and I look forward to your return"…"Jesus, be with Julie and keep her safe and bring her home soon"…"I will miss collecting the eggs with you"…"I will miss cooking with you"…"God bless and take care of you, Julie."

Almost everyone in the room had something to say. Michael Allen, especially, perhaps because of the number of times he himself had been jailed, was extremely sensitive and compassionate in a way that enriched the spirit of the entire evening. It was one of the few occasions when he did not hesitate to play the guitar, something he often did when alone but rarely in public. His gentle, self-taught manner of playing was always peace-giving. An awesome stillness filled the room as he played and sang in almost a whisper "Hang Down Your Head, Tom Dooley." Only Michael with his prayerful spirit could in such a situation sing a song about a man about to be executed for stabbing a woman to death and have it bring peace to the group. There were more than a few tears as we ended the vigil by each of us hugging Julie and one another.

Later that evening there was a shift from sadness to joy as people gathered around Byron and me in our bedroom to welcome us home and to receive the souvenir T-shirts we had brought back for each member of the community. People were surprised to hear us already talking about our next trip.

* * * * *

MEANWHILE, BACK AT THE RANCH

Dear Mum and Dad,

The rector of Ignatius College, who actually likes the Farm Community and believes in it, came over to say mass in our living room today because Bill and Byron have gone to Acapulco. There's a lovely Down's Syndrome boy called Mark who comes to mass here sometimes. He adores priests. He always sits beside Bill and Bill allows him to practically run the show. Bill not being here, Mark sat beside the rector all the same, a rather dry stick who seems much older than his actual age of 50. Mark imitated all his liturgical gestures the entire way through, and at times corrected them. When the priest stretched out his arms to bless the bread and wine, Mark would reach out and correct his arm level, or adjust one or two fingers that he considered were sticking out too much. When there was nothing to copy he stroked his hair. It was wonderful. I'm sure no one has stroked the guy's hair since his mother died 45 years ago.

———

August 2, 1987

We have been making hay like crazy. We have had wonderful growing weather, although a lot of it almost unbearably humid and the second cut of hay is very lush. Yesterday I spent five hours on the tractor cutting about 20 acres of hay. I came back with my back muscles so tense that it affected my brain and I couldn't talk for about an hour. Then this morning I woke up to the sound of a deluge of rain, which is normally such a wonderful cozy sound but after you've just cut a field of hay it doesn't sound so good.

We are starting the Companion Orientation tonight. Bill is miserable, as he always is before the orientation, because it means three weeks or so away from home. He sits glumly in front of the TV trying to get excited over the baseball scores.

Lots of love,
Weesa

12

By the Grace of God and a Wooden Spoon

The summer following our trip to Mexico was a typical summer at the community, very full and busy for all of us.

On the first Sunday of June was the traditional land blessing, celebrated by about 40 adults and a number of children, community members and friends, who all gathered on this lovely morning in the driveway of the Farm House to begin the event. After a spirited time of greeting each other we began with a hymn, "God Whose Farm Is All Creation," led by Weesa playing the guitar. Then, wearing an astonishing array of caps, straw hats and bonnets to protect us from the bright sun, we all climbed onto the two hay wagons, which had been carefully furnished with three tiers of straw bales so that everyone could sit in relative comfort. With Tom driving one tractor and Pat the other, we set out to tour the farm, stopping at a number of points along the way so that different people could say a prayer of blessing on the barns, the pigs, the stream and pond, the fields and field crops, the hermitages, the wildlife, the trees, the fences, the cattle, the vegetable gardens, the sheep and goats, the barns and barn cats, the apple orchard, the apple storage and root cellar, and so forth and so on, and finally our homes and the people who live in them.

Brother Jim Deshaye, a man of great gentleness who had been living in the Red House for a couple of years, blessed the trees in a spirit of loving reverence:

> Lord, we ask you to bless the trees, for they give great beauty to the land; as well, they provide most delicious fruit. They also provide what is needed for us to build our homes, and they provide fuel for heat. They give a safe place where birds and squirrels may rest, and they shelter these and many other living things. They shade us from the summer sun and give shade to the cattle and many other kinds of animals; they shelter us and animals from winds strong and cold. They help to keep soil from being carried away by wind and they benefit the crops. They supply us and many kinds of your creatures with nourishing food: apples, pears, plums, maple syrup, and so on. Please keep them safe from disease, fire, storm and whatever else may harm them. Amen.

Mary's blessing of the pigs was not so solemn:

> God bless these pigs, and make them stay in their friggin' pens and not go running around messing up the barn, and make them hurry up and get fat because we're out of pork chops. Amen.

Tim Lilburn's blessing reveals that same talent that has made him the accomplished and acclaimed poet of today:

> Lord, bless our tools and equipment. These are more than steel, rubber, grease, cast iron, pans of oil, wood. They are the real presence of human genius, for the minds and hands of other women and men have made these tools, this equipment to be extensions of the creative human spirit that tills soil, feeds animals, hoes weeds. Bless, Lord, bless these tools; through them we are co-creators; may we use them with respect; may we use them in your service.

With each blessing, the person praying or one of the children with a cedar bough would splash water from a bucket in the direction of whatever was being blessed. All was done in a spirit of joyful solemnity and also good fun as water was splashed with excessive exuberance to be sure that people along with fields, livestock and so on got a good dousing. A short thanksgiving refrain was sung after each blessing or group of blessings. The hay ride took us through many beautiful areas of the property as well as one swampy area where we became breakfast for clouds of ravenous mosquitoes. It terminated in a corner of one of the apple orchards which was in glorious blossom. There we moved our straw bales from the wagons into a circle on the ground, and with two bales for an altar and the refreshing incense of apple blossoms, we celebrated the Sunday liturgy with enthusiastic if not melodious singing. A barbecue lunch brought the happy event to a fitting conclusion. These celebrations helped us gain a deepening appreciation for the gift of our farm and our vocation to be sensitive, co-operative partners and just stewards of this gift.

Byron had a deep love for the land but he was not up to participating in this celebration. However, he certainly enjoyed the hamburgers, potato salad and apple pie that I took back to the house for him. Shortly after this he came down with another bad attack of bronchitis, and was put on antibiotics. The antibiotics, as usual, put him deeper into depression and this eventually led to his drinking again. It had been about nine months since his last stay in the Homewood Psychiatric Hospital to get help with his depression and addiction. Perhaps it was the work he had done there that helped him get through this present bout of drinking in just a few days.

He was also being buoyed up by the hope of getting dentures, even though it involved a complicated procedure of having titanium posts implanted into his jaw to which the dentures could be attached. I did my best not to show my concern about having holes drilled into this fragile jaw constructed out of bone from his hip. We went to Mount Sinai Hospital in Toronto a few weeks later, where the doctor did all the necessary tests on Byron's jaw. He concluded that the operation could be done without any great risk, but that the resulting dentures would be purely cosmetic and would not be a help for eating. By this time Byron had become more accepting of his appearance but nevertheless he was eager for whatever could be done by way of improvement.

The implant surgery was a long, drawn-out process that involved many visits to the hospital, with each implant being done separately and needing a number of weeks for the healing and bonding that had to take place between the jaw bone and the implanted post. This was at times very painful, but Byron rarely complained and to my surprise did not give in to discouragement. Once the implants were completed there were many visits to a special dental clinic. I was amazed at his determination to see it through to the end. It was almost a year before Byron was proudly sporting his brand new dentures.

They did indeed make some minor improvement to his appearance, enough for him to feel that it was all worth the pain and trouble. With his upper lip filled out better he had less problem with his nose slipping down over his lip, and his infectious smile became almost glamorous. Getting the dentures into place was a very tricky manoeuvre because of the limited opening of his mouth. I found I was twisting my own jaw out of joint just watching him do this, so for my own well-being I had to avoid seeing that particular daily performance.

This was the summer that Byron taught Liz to drive. Liz (Sr. Elizabeth Budicky) came to the Farm Community several years after Byron and me, and what a gift she was with her years of formation as a Sister of St. Joseph, her training as a nurse and her many years of experience in nursing and hospital administration. It was no small transition for Liz to move into the Farm House with the mess and chaos of our lives spilling out into every room of the house to mingle with the mess that got dragged in from the farm each day on our boots and clothes. With her strong sense of duty, she met the challenge with great courage and determination and managed to stick it out with us for four years.

Farming was not totally foreign to her, as she had grown up on a farm in southern Ontario, but it would take some time for the farm girl to re-emerge from the heavy overlay of religious and professional formation. When it came to butchering chickens, for example, there was no one better than Liz at catching them. She would already be carrying two or three out of the pen by the legs while I was still trying to corner and grab my first, even though as an ex-boxer with the University of Toronto I had pretty quick hands and good footwork. I was hampered in the pen in the same way as I had been in the ring; my gentle spirit made me fearful of hurting my opponents, whether they had flailing wings and feathers or flailing arms and boxing gloves. Liz was also great at the rest of the process of butchering and cleaning. But one would have to say that order and cleanliness remained very important to Liz, in deed and word and, I would surmise, in thought as well. As unlikely a match as it was, she and Byron got on very well together.

Liz had a good sense of humour but she was not one for telling jokes. She did tell one funny story that became legendary, only because it was Liz who told it. It was the story of Molly and her drunkard of a husband, Mike. Every Saturday night Mike would come home dead drunk, stagger over to the kitchen sink and throw up everything, retching violently. Molly would be furious with him and scold him, saying, "If you keep this up, one day you're going to end up by retching up your whole insides." So one Saturday evening, Molly was cleaning a chicken. Just as she got out all its guts into the kitchen sink the phone in the living room rang. She returned from her phone conversation to discover Mike all glassy-eyed standing by the sink. "Well," said Mike, "it finally happened. I retched up all my guts into the kitchen sink – but by the grace of God and a wooden spoon I managed to get them all back in again."

What made the story especially funny was that Liz would cry with laughter as she told it, and we made her tell it over and over again. *By the grace of God and a wooden spoon* became a catchphrase in the community for years afterwards.

Since Liz did more than her share of cooking, Byron took the time one day to share with her his recipe for cooking groundhog. Our farm is plagued with hundreds of them which Byron and I would occasionally hunt but no one would ever think of eating. Byron began explaining very carefully to her just how to go about it:

"Take a big cast iron pot, put in the groundhog and cover it with water; throw in a few onions and carrots, and lots of salt and pepper. Boil it for at least five hours. Then take out the groundhog, throw the damn thing away, and eat the pot."

Because of her friendship with Byron, Liz accepted his invitation to teach her to drive a car. She probably did not realize what she was getting herself into.

During those lessons, Liz heard more foul language than she would have heard in all her previous life and that she would want to hear in the rest of her life, but she sure learned how to drive. Once I was in the back seat while Liz was getting a driving lesson on Highway 401. Byron knew that if she could drive on that multi-lane raceway, she could drive anywhere. It was raining hard, the traffic was heavy and Byron was urging her to pass a transport truck. Of course she was getting very nervous and so was I as the huge truck was sending up a dense curtain of spray. Byron was in his element, and kept saying, "Don't back off, Liz, don't back off." Since she passed that test, in Byron's opinion, she was ready for her driving test. She went to take the test quite confident that she would pass.

We were all waiting in the kitchen to congratulate her on her return, but as soon as she stepped into the house, I could tell by the look on her face that it was not good news. They had failed her on some silly technical detail, and Liz was not a happy camper. She was trying to tell us how angry she felt but her convent language just hadn't provided her with the vocabulary. "I'm, I'm, I'm…" she was desperately searching for the right word, and finally she exclaimed to the applause of all of us, "I'm pissed off!" Byron's lessons were not just about driving. I think it was fortunate for the man who tested Liz the second time that he found no reason to fail her.

One September morning I received a phone call from Wayne, who had been away from the community for over six months. For much of this time he had been living in Cornwall to be close to his mother. He called to inform me that she had died during the night, and asked me to perform the funeral rites. I didn't need another thing to do but felt honoured to be asked. Later that day in the context of the Sunday liturgy, presided by Doug, we had the baptism of Stash, the first child of Paul and Halinka, whose wedding had taken place here on the Farm a year earlier. As a community of farmers we were used to death and new life being juxtaposed. The next day, September 8, which happened to be the 30th anniversary of my entrance into the Jesuits, I set out for Cornwall carrying a number of cards and messages of sympathy for Wayne and his family.

Wayne's mother, Shirley, had been a broken little woman who had not had an easy go of it. She lived much of her life on welfare, which could hardly support her addiction to alcohol let alone her seven children when they were with her. None of the relationships with the various fathers of her children had survived. In Wayne's early days in the community his mother took advantage of him, taking most of his meagre earnings from part-time work with the Humane Society and other occasional odd jobs. However, he always remained very attached and devoted to her.

I was touched by how noble Shirley looked lying in her coffin, the turmoil of her life finally over. I learned later that this was the very day that she and Wayne were to have appeared in court on a charge of shoplifting. Four of Wayne's sisters were there, as well as his brother and his brother's girlfriend and her mother. It seemed that all of the children were very attached to their mother, given the outpouring of grief they demonstrated. The prayer service that I began that evening was washed out in a flood of tears. At the funeral service the next day we were helped by the stabilizing presence of two men from the local Catholic church who led the music, and by a few aunts and uncles from Montreal who disappeared after the service almost as quickly as they had appeared before it. Later that day, at my insistence, Wayne drove back to the community with me after picking up his few belongings from a rooming house and seeing his lawyer about a new trial date. I was deeply moved by his silent tears and happy for him that on our arrival at the Farm House he received such an affectionate welcome from Byron, Liz and Mary the Russian Princess, the only ones home at the time.

Whenever I returned home after being away from the community for a while, my feelings would usually be a mixture of dread and gratitude. One Sunday later that month, driving home after a weekend away, as the Farm House came into view I heaved my usual sigh of relief: "Thank God the house is still standing; it hasn't been burned down or blown up." There were other days when that first sigh of relief would be followed by a sense of dread and a desire to just keep on driving. I remember on that particular day pulling into the driveway with a deep sense of gratitude: "It's good to be home."

Stepping out of the car on this pleasant evening, I was greeted anxiously by Rick, a friend of the community who had been staying with us for several months. He informed me that Jake, the bull, had come across the swamp and was threatening to leap the fence that was keeping him from a group of heifers, some of which were in heat but were too young to be bred.

I went with Rick to assess the situation. There was Jake, this young but very powerful black beast, pacing back and forth along the fence line, his nose in the air, lustfully sniffing the sweet young virgins on the other side.

What to do? Driving an infatuated bull back through or around the swamp to his own herd was unlikely to succeed, given the nature of the swamp and the long route around it through a number of gates and across several fields. The solution seemed obvious and relatively simple; just lock him in the nearby barn for the night. In the morning with a full work crew we could easily get Jake back where he belonged.

I called Joe away from a crib game with Byron, thinking that one more person might be helpful for the task at hand. Joe, a Jesuit student from Oregon, was spending the summer with us.

"I could throw him over my shoulder and carry him across the swamp the way I did last time he got out," offered Byron generously.

"Thanks, Pal," I said. "I know you don't like to do that kind of work on Sunday."

"I'm not the biggest liar in the world," he said with a wink, "but I'm one of the top two."

As we were leaving he gave us some sobering advice. "You'd better be careful; there's no such thing as a harmless bull."

Joe and I headed into the field towards Jake, while Rick waited by the corral gate ready to close it as soon as we got Jake to go through. I instinctively grabbed a big stick that happened to be lying by the fence, and in doing so became aware of my mounting fear. Just purchased in the spring, this bull was still an unknown quantity. Could he be mean? Could he turn on us? He had not shown any signs of viciousness, but one never knows. I could see that Jake was angry and frustrated. His own herd was back across the swamp. The young heifers whose scent had drawn him seemed to be deliberately taunting him from the other side of the fence. Jake was poised for action.

I reconsidered the decision. Was it wise to approach this unpredictable power that was capable of seriously injuring or even killing someone? Rick called out a hesitant warning: "Uh, uh…maybe this is too dangerous." Joe was new in the community and was relying on my experience. Little did he know how limited this was. For a moment I hesitated, but then assuring myself that in my seven years on the farm no one had ever been hurt by a bull, I clutched my cedar club more firmly and advanced.

Jake was moving away on a little slope above me. When I got to within 30 feet of him, he turned to face me, lowering his massive head and prodding the dusty earth. Images from the bullfights I had seen years ago in Spain flashed before me: magnificent, lethal monsters charging mounted picadors and heaving them and their horses into the air and over the barrier; catching matadors with a flick of their powerful heads and then turning on their fallen victims to maul and maim them.

As he started towards me, I thought of Byron's parting words. Would they be the last words I'd ever hear from him? I made an instant assessment: the fence off to the left was twice the distance that was rapidly diminishing between Jake and me – I'd never make it. If I did bolt towards safety, Joe, some 10 feet to my right, would be more endangered. The pile of cedar rails behind us could afford some protection but again it was too far. Only one hope remained.

Desperation gave me courage. There was no time or space left to entertain my fears. I started shouting, raised my club, and, like a banderillero in a bullfight, charged.

I was immensely relieved to see Jake slow his pace then turn away. He could still decide to attack but for now we had him on the run. Twice we had him headed towards the corral gate, but both times he turned away and circled us again. On the third attempt we managed to steer him through the gate, which Rick quickly closed. Fortunately, after only one angry circle around the corral, Jake charged into the barn, and we raced to roll the doors closed behind him. Success! Well, almost.

Once inside the barn, Jake became more enraged. He spurned the grain and hay placed in the manger to appease him. Round and round the pen he stormed, sometimes testing the strength of the big barn doors, which heaved and creaked but held.

We checked the closures on the doors and started to leave, assuming that he would eventually simmer down, but we had only taken a few steps towards the house when CRASH! Right through one of the doors he went, reducing it to splinters. Pride, power and rage did a turn around the corral, leaped the four-and-a-half-foot cedar rail fence and was free. The three of us watched in awe as this splendid animal, on his own terms with head held high, moved back into the swamp to join the cows on the other side. I offered a silent prayer of thanksgiving that it was only a barn door that had been smashed by this not so harmless young bull.

Back in the house I was more than ready to take on Byron at crib, a game in which only my pride could be hurt. While the game proceeded I recounted my near-death experience and how by the grace of God and a wooden stick we had managed to get Jake into the barn. After attentively taking in the whole story, Byron shook his head slowly, then said even more slowly, "Sometimes you win but sometimes you lose."

"I was just taking your advice, Pal," I said, not wanting the episode to end on a worrisome note. "You always say *come big or stay home.* I guess Jake took it, too. Maybe when we get to Spain we can go to a bullfight."

"I'm finding it hard to believe that I'm really going to France and Spain with you," he said, accepting the change of subject.

"You're coming, Pal, and we're going to have a great time."

"But the only French I know is *bonjour, comment ça va,* and the only Spanish I know is *adios.*"

"Well, that's perfect; it's all you need to arrive and to leave, and in between you'll be among friends." I was speaking confidently but actually was not really sure myself how it was all going to work out. I did have a gut feeling that it would, even though the friends who were to welcome us had also been expressing some concern.

For me there remained only one major project to bring this summer to an end and to enter into the season of autumn, at the heart of which would be our trip to Europe.

What I had yet to do and was looking forward to was my annual eight-day retreat, a time of solitude, prayer and reflection that is part of our Jesuit way of life. Ordinarily, I would spend these eight days during the month of May in our hermitage, a little cabin in an isolated corner of the farm. This year I was too overwhelmed with all that was happening here in the spring to feel free to get away. Also, it seemed important for me with all that I had lived this past year to have the support of a friend and guide and not be simply alone – albeit in the company of God. So I had decided to go to Omaha, Nebraska, in order to be with my dear friend and fellow Jesuit Fr. Larry Gillick.

During the retreat I followed the usual pattern of praying with the mysteries of the life of Jesus. A little less usual was the watching of a lot of high school football. Larry was the superior of Creighton Prep Jesuit High School and an avid supporter of the football teams. On the fourth day of my retreat I watched the senior team, trailing 14–7, tie the game in the last 50 seconds of regular play, and then win it in overtime 17–14 by a field goal. In the locker room afterwards the coach led his players in reciting the Hail Mary and praised them for their gutsy refusal to give up.

I can't say that this greatly nourished my retreat prayer, but I, too, realized that I needed some gutsiness to resist the temptation to give up since my prayer was not going very well. The game took me back to my own high school days of playing football. I remembered how I played well in official competitions but brilliantly when it was just for fun with the neighbourhood guys on the weekends. This brought home to me the importance of having fun to bring out the best in me, and as a way for me to encounter God in my life and in my relationships with others. I gave thanks for the fun times with Byron and with others in the community as well as for my friend Larry and the ways he helps me to have fun.

Often in the late morning we would go for a jog around the track. Since Larry is blind, he managed to do this by hanging on to a string attached to my arm. Once a group of African-American students from another school were watching us jog, and we heard one of them announce, "I want to get me one of them – a white boy on a string."

I may have been doing some fun things but I was still hanging in with my retreat. At this point I was trying to pray with the mystery of the suffering and death of Jesus but was having trouble getting into it. Finally I realized that I was being invited rather to pray with the Resurrection. It seemed that I had experienced enough suffering and death already in the past year and a half, so I began to contemplate the Risen Lord going to comfort his mother and the disciples. Soon I had the experience of him coming to comfort me.

In this comforting embrace of the Lord I began to sob uncontrollably, getting in touch with the wounds and the pain that I had experienced but had not the freedom to acknowledge and grieve at the time: the painful fallout from Harry's accident; the suffering and departure of the O'Connor family; other difficult departures and difficult relationships; and my confusion, fear and loneliness associated with Byron's drinking as well as his cancer and deteriorating health. For the next two days I tried to turn away from or minimize my own pain in the light of how much these others had suffered and continued to suffer, but Larry kept gently encouraging me to face the truth of my own suffering and allow the Risen Lord to comfort me. So I did my best to stay with my own hurts and loneliness. There was, for example, the struggle with a young woman who had been with us for two years as a Jesuit Companion. It was clear to me and to others that her decision to leave and return to college was right. Then, at the last minute, she said she had had a deep religious experience in which Jesus was telling her that she needed to stay for another year. In spite of my own doubts and fear of wounding her, I had to insist that maybe Jesus was telling her to stay but I was telling her she needed to go, and in this case it was I and not Jesus who had the final say. It was always painful for me to have to ask or at least encourage someone to leave. On the other hand, when Paul left it was a different kind of pain. During his year with us he had become a very dear friend, and since he, like me, was a civil engineer, we had worked together on a number of projects, such as some major repairs to the barn. Rarely in the community had I experienced such strong peer companionship, and his departure left a deep emptiness in me that was compounded when Byron withdrew into alcohol. Every departure, and there were many, wounded me in one way or another. Nor could I be indifferent to the deep suffering of others in the community, all of which entered into me and became my pain as well, perhaps to a lesser degree but nevertheless in a very real way. With the support, encouragement and companionship of my friend Larry I was able to enter into the sacred space of grief and remain there for a couple of days. I shed copious tears, and I felt the tender, compassionate embrace of Jesus, which released even more tears. In the end I experienced a peace and freedom the likes of which I had not known in the preceding two or three years.

There was no doubt in my mind that I was in the right place living in the Farm Community – indeed, it was a great privilege – but I had to acknowledge that I was paying a price for this unique gift.

★ ★ ★ ★ ★

MEANWHILE, BACK AT THE RANCH

October 4, 1985

Dear Mum and Dad,

I'm having a hard time adjusting to sharing a room full-time. My roommate is a Sister of St. Joseph called Elizabeth Budicky – Liz. She is very nice but overwhelmed by the dirt and slovenliness of the house. She is beginning to be very vocal in her criticisms of how we live. The last thing I feel like getting excited about right now is cleaning the house, with the piles of grain, silage, hay, manure, birthing cows, etc., that need dealing with outside. Liz was so upset by the odd fly that strays into our bedroom that she hung up one of those disgusting yellow spirals of sticky fly-murdering paper, right in the window, so that the other evening when I was standing looking out, probably trying to appreciate the beauty that must be out there if only I wasn't too tired to see it, I got my hair stuck in the fly-paper. I should have waited until Liz came in and said, "Look what you caught,

Liz! The biggest disease carrier in the house!" (Ever since I came back from living in Nepal I have been inhabited by various intestinal parasites.) One of these nights I'll entertain her with stories of what the Tropical Diseases Hospital found in my gut. She grew up on a farm but has been working in a hospital and living in a convent for years, so it must be quite an adjustment. I'm trying to keep my room tidy. Her side looks like a hotel room before the guests arrive. Every time I walk into the room I look at my side and then at her side and then her side and then my side again, and an anxious knot grips my stomach. Or perhaps it's the tapeworm.

Love from
Weesa

———

February 1986

Dear Mum and Dad,

I'm sitting right beside the stove, as it is quite cold in the house. Liz is kneeling on the floor trying to shove a piece of cardboard into the stove. Liz seems to really be in her element now. After all those years in hospitals and convents, now when you see her on her knees building a fire or with her arms in a chicken degutting it, or collecting the eggs from the chicken coop, you know she has come home. She has not abandoned her battle to raise the cleanliness standards here, however. We no longer share a room and that has improved our friendship. She has the most delightful and outrageous sense of humour, which seems to be emerging from remission. Now she often laughs so much that she can't speak. She also has a deep faith and wisdom that knocks me out. The nerve of her, to move here after all those safe, secure and predictable years. I admire it very much and hope I would have the courage to do such a thing at her age.

Love from

Weesa

———————

April 1987

I spent a lot of my day tidying my room because it was getting difficult to reach my bed. Then I took Liz in to see it. She looked around and smiled a bit confusedly and then said, "Did you do anything constructive today?"

Oh, well.

Spring is springing right now, just bursting. It is so exhilarating to turn the soil and smell the fresh earth. I dug up the garden with a roto-tiller and found a baby toad and a mother toad. The baby toad peed on me. The swamp is deafening with the song of snipe and killdeer and red-winged blackbird, and the blue heron lifts from it every morning when we pass on the way to the shop. We have finally finished planting everything except the corn. I love it here more and more and wonder every day why I'm leaving. I'm going to mourn terribly.

Bill is squealing in a very high voice, involuntarily, because he just got a good hand in crib against Byron.

Lots of love,

Weesa

13

I Missed You So Much I Couldn't Stay Away

In the days just before our trip to Europe, Byron would often sing repeatedly the opening bars of "O Canada," replacing the "O" with "Air." We were both so excited about the prospect of making this trip together that we went shopping at the St. Vincent de Paul and Salvation Army thrift stores to upgrade our wardrobes. After all, we were going to Paris, Barcelona and Madrid.

Making a fashion statement was not really foremost in our minds, but the damp weather we might encounter was of great concern for both of us since we would be so far away from our dear friend, the wood stove. Coincidentally, on the day before we left I spent the morning with a work crew packing the woodshed of the Farm House with hard, dry firewood, and the rest of the day putting the storm windows on the house. That evening we had no trouble packing into our carry-on bags everything we were taking – including, of course, a crib board and cards. Then, with Byron chanting "Air Canada," we played a few games of crib to ready our spirits for the journey.

Returning to the original l'Arche community in France was always a moving experience for me. This was the place where I was given a much deeper acceptance of myself, a greater freedom to be me. This was the place where I had been renewed in a simpler and more personal relationship with Jesus, a relationship that was more mature and at the same time closer to how it had been when I was a child. It was the experience that in many ways gave shape to the way I would be a priest and live out this ministry of service and compassion as a companion of Jesus. It was because of my time in l'Arche, where I discovered more about God's predilection for the poor, that I was now living in the Farm Community. So I was going home, returning to very important spiritual roots and to many dear friends who would eagerly welcome me and my friend and lavish us with love and kindness.

The seven-and-a-half-hour flight to Paris went very quickly. Byron took extra time to stuff down the large dinner as well as the breakfast that was served and to drink several coffees. Intersperse these with a few crib games, a nap, and before long it was time to fasten our seatbelts for the landing at Charles de Gaulle airport. Byron was thrilled to be arriving in France, and I was even more thrilled to be sharing this aspect of my life with him.

Two friends met us at the airport, one of whom, Dave Rothrock, had met Byron several times during visits to the Farm Community. Immediately my worries about how Byron would manage in a foreign culture vanished.

Part of the one-hour drive to the l'Arche community in the little town of Trosly-Breuil, north of Paris, was through the magnificent Compiègne forest, scenery that always moves my heart to gratitude. Eagerly I turned to point this out to Byron, but found he was fast asleep.

On arrival we were taken directly to our rooms upstairs in *les Marronniers*, the home of Madame Vanier, Jean's mother, the same house where I lodged from 1969–71 while I was working on my thesis. Madame Vanier, affectionately known as "Mammy," welcomed us with her usual graciousness. The welcome of the community was extended to us minutes later with the arrival of Barbara and Françoise. Barbara, Jean Vanier's secretary (the term is inadequate since she fills many roles and seems to embody the very spirit of l'Arche) has been here since 1965, the year after the community was founded. She was the one who picked me up at the nearby train station on my first visit to l'Arche in 1968. Françoise was at that time in charge of the workshop where I spent part of that memorable month working alongside people whose gifts were primarily in the realm of relationships and not efficiency. After some good French *café au lait* we went with Barbara for a stroll through the village, meeting many old friends along the way. One of these was someone who had been asking for weeks, "*Quand est-ce que le Père Clarke arrive?*" (When is Fr. Clarke arriving?) I met Pierrot in 1968, when we worked together in the bookbinding workshop under the supervision of Françoise. He lit up when he saw me and gave me a loving embrace, showing similar kindness to Byron. Pierrot's unwaning faithfulness and tenderness over these many years symbolizes for me the very tenderness and faithfulness of God.

As a light rain began we returned to *les Marronniers* in time for a game of crib before joining Mammy for lunch. Byron sat with us briefly, then went to his room to lie down and eat. When I went upstairs an hour later, I gently removed the empty plate from his chest and left him to snore on for another two hours while I took my own siesta. We had afternoon tea with Mammy and a friend, after which I left Byron and Mammy together for an hour while I went for a walk. The two of them got on famously, since this noble woman had such a deep love for people and an especially tender place in her heart for those who had obviously been wounded in one way or another, and Byron had his own charm. That evening Jean came to greet us and join us for supper with his mother, something he rarely finds time to do.

We contentedly ended our first day by playing a couple of games of crib. Byron shared how touched he was by the warmth and kindness he was receiving, and I was happy to affirm how he was winning the hearts of those he was meeting.

Scattered through this village of a couple of hundred houses, l'Arche has half a dozen homes, as well as a few homes in the neighbouring villages. There are also a number of lodgings for assistants who, for lack of space or other reasons, do not live in the homes. There is a large workshop, a meeting hall and a chapel that was once an old stone barn. Then there is *la Ferme*, a kind of small, contemplative community of prayer and welcome at the heart of l'Arche. This was founded under the inspiration of Père Thomas with a view to helping the whole community stay rooted in faith and prayer.

Byron and I had most of our meals at the *Val Fleuri*, the largest and oldest home in the community, which for me is something of a home away from home. Some of the residents here I had known for over 20 years. Most of them knew no English, but they were used to welcoming and communicating with people from many different cultures. This was a fun time as Byron tried on a few French words he was learning and they pulled out their limited repertoire of English. Some of the residents here have little or no verbal skills, so for them the distinction between French and English is of lesser importance. One man in this home, though he has excellent verbal skills, at one point had simply decided that it was better for him to communicate without the use of words. He has continued in this resolve not to speak for over 10 years now, with the exception of the occasional visit from his domineering mother, who insists that her son act "normally." Fasting from the use of words has made this man much more peaceful and communicative. Byron, for three or more years following his accident, had his own experience of fasting from the use of spoken language, but that was anything but peaceful.

Nevertheless, that painful experience ultimately contributed to his deepening compassion and understanding of vulnerable people.

One afternoon in Mammy's living room I celebrated mass in English for her and a dozen people who were grateful to participate at mass in their own language for a change. My friend Pierrot was there, beaming with joy through the entire hour, even though he could only recognize the occasional word, such as *Jesus*, and *peace be with you*. That evening Pierrot welcomed Byron and me to his home for supper, along with Michel from the home next door. Michel is another incredibly faithful friend who has been praying for me daily since we met in 1968, a meeting that was unforgettable. We spent a month of summer vacation together during a period in Michel's life when the only way he knew how to relate to people was to annoy them. The more he liked a person, the more developed and insistent were his tactics of annoyance, and Michel liked me most of all. He has changed his ways of relating since then but his love for me has remained constant.

In Mammy's kitchen we gratefully concluded another good day, playing crib while carrying on a delightful and animated conversation with David, Ted, a Canadian Jesuit and good friend of the Farm Community, and Alain, the director of l'Arche, Trosly, who had also been to the Farm.

Claire, a vivacious woman in her late 30s, picked us up early the next morning to drive us to Tressaint, a centre in Brittany where I was going to preach a Covenant Retreat to about 50 l'Arche assistants, the principal reason for my coming to France. It was Claire who had translated into French my book about l'Arche and who is the translator of Jean's book *Drawn into the Mystery of Jesus through the Gospel of John*. Only those who were long-term, committed members of l'Arche communities were invited to participate in a Covenant Retreat, six days of prayer and faith sharing to help the participants deepen in their vocation to live in l'Arche. Byron's presence was very much an exception; however, given our relationship, he was warmly welcomed as a guest of honour.

Claire speaks impeccable English, so the three of us were able to converse freely during the five-hour trip that took us around Paris and through some lovely countryside and numerous little villages. When we arrived, she very generously volunteered to translate for Byron each of my two daily conferences.

In my opening conference I told the retreatants that I had brought along a companion to help me prepare my talks, something we would be doing faithfully every evening by playing cards. Everyone laughed. Moments later, after Claire's translation, Byron also chuckled, which brought forth a second round of laughter. I made the statement facetiously by way of introducing Byron and inviting the people to relax into the coming days, but I and the others quickly began to discover how true it was. In fact, it was not just evenings, but also in free moments during the day that we played crib, and this time together was, strangely enough, excellent preparation for my talks. As the week unfolded I told a number of humorous stories about life in the Farm Community, each one getting a double round of laughter, with Byron's delayed chuckles sandwiched in between as a kind of verification of the authenticity of each story. It was becoming clear to me and everyone else, with the exception of Byron, perhaps, that it was the two of us who were preaching this retreat.

Since this was a Covenant Retreat, I spoke about various aspects of the covenant as it is understood and lived in l'Arche. This covenant, a gift from God, is a friendship or a bonding of faithfulness to Jesus and to all the brothers and sisters in l'Arche, especially those weakest and most fragile members who are at the heart of the community. Jesus invites people into l'Arche not simply to be of service but rather to live relationships of mutuality. Often we discover in these relationships that it is the person who appears to be the most limited and needy who can be most open to the loving presence of God, who *is* relationship, and so can strongly call others into deeper unity within themselves and with the divine. In this context I could readily speak about the covenant that I had been invited to live with Jesus and with all my brothers and sisters in the Farm Community – especially Byron and others who were also deeply wounded and vulnerable. Even as I preached this retreat with Byron, I was becoming more conscious and appreciative of what a precious gift he was in my life, and how much our covenant was leading me into a deeper relationship with Jesus. Our relationship was mutually bringing healing and life to us and to others in the Farm Community. This covenant that Byron and I were living was not just a gift contained within the Farm Community but, as we were experiencing here in France, to many others as well.

I thought it important to speak to this group about the countercultural nature of l'Arche and the Farm Community. Immersed as most of them were in the dailiness of getting their people out of bed, helping them with baths and hygiene routines, meal preparations, housekeeping and so forth, accompanying them in workshops, gardens, shopping, various appointments and the like, they could easily lose sight of the bigger picture. Through these mundane tasks they were drawn into ever-deepening and mutually life-giving heart-to-heart relationships. They would, however, not always receive support and encouragement from their families and friends outside of l'Arche. What they were living in these fragile little communities could seem from the outside a waste of time and talent. In fact, they were giving witness that every human being is unique and precious, no matter how limited they may seem to be, and that the human project is really all about relationship, not about power and wealth. In this sense such communities are greatly needed signs of hope in today's world.

Even now as I reflect upon who Byron was for me, I see a little deeper into the gift of our relationship and the secret of his life. It relates to the mystery of how the presence of God can be revealed and discovered more readily through vulnerability and suffering. God, who is loving each one of us into existence at every moment and for all eternity, is always lovingly present in each one of us and in and through our love for one another. This divine presence is, for the most part, very hidden, since God creates us out of love and freedom in order that we might freely respond in love. You might say that we are loved into being with no strings attached. Mysteriously, God's presence seems to be least clearly revealed in our strengths and capacities, since by these we can tend to be little gods rather than God's children humbly receiving our lives as the gifts that they truly are. The deepest, truest human freedom is the freedom to love and to gratefully receive everything as gift. Jesus rejoiced that this truth, this freedom was especially accessible to the little ones, those who are or who are like little children: "I thank you, Father, Lord of heaven and earth, for although you have hidden these things from the wise and the learned you have revealed them to the childlike" (Luke 10:21). The infant in its mother's womb, if carried in love, has a sense, a pre-cognitive awareness, of lovingly receiving its being. The touch of God who is Love that gives breath and life to the tiny being in the womb already marks that being as destined for Love. And that tiny being in the womb can already give so much life to its mother. Most of us in our journey into adulthood necessarily develop our physical and intellectual strengths, learn to defend ourselves and grow in independence. In that process we can abandon our childlikeness and build protective barriers around our ever-vulnerable hearts, losing the sense that we are created by Love and for Love. The people with severe intellectual disabilities, like those at the heart of l'Arche, make little progress in this growth process, remaining always very dependent with their hearts more defenceless and open. The vocation of l'Arche is to foster communities of faith and love that nurture these vulnerable hearts so that they can open to the

God of love, who alone can sound the depths of the heart and who longs to communicate with each one of us, heart to heart. In this way these vulnerable ones, dear to the heart of God, can grow in holiness and offer their gifts of tenderness, fidelity and forgiveness to our needy world.

For those of us who have developed our strengths and gained autonomy and independence, it is often only the journey into old age or into illness that teaches us the fundamental truth that we are always radically in need of others and of the Other, the Source of our existence. Somehow, when the human person, through old age or illness or the suffering of humiliation and rejection, is reduced to the barest essentials of existence, the divine presence is more readily revealed. This wondrous mystery is the foundation of l'Arche and of the Farm Community, communities that are founded on suffering, founded in response to deep human pain. These are communities that by their very nature are destined to remain fragile and vulnerable and with much pain, and that cannot easily ignore their deep and constant need for God. Such communities, like the individuals within them, are earthen vessels containing precious treasure.

But could it be true that God would be more readily revealed in someone like Byron, who to a large extent brought suffering on himself, and inflicted terrible pain on others? He deeply grieved the suffering he had caused to his family and himself; this very grief was part of the pain that made him more vulnerable and more aware of his poverty and need. Whatever the source of his suffering, he did journey downward into human weakness and humiliation in a way that reduced him to the bare necessity of human existence. All of this did make him somehow more transparent to the inner truth of what it is to be human and to receive one's being from Another. He was certainly leading me to a deeper encounter with God, who is both hidden and revealed in our poverty.

189

The weather in France was, as I had feared, very damp, with rain almost every day, so it was not long before both of us started coming down with colds. However, it was not primarily the weather that dampened Byron's spirit. In the middle of the retreat we had an "evening with our people," a time to remember and give thanks for the people at the heart of the l'Arche communities, the people with whom the retreatants felt called into covenant relationships. This was done mainly by showing slides of these people, many of them with severe handicaps but with such beautiful faces revealing aspects of the face of God. The invitation to remember and give thanks for people who had deeply touched our lives raised up in Byron memories of his wife and daughters, reopening the painful wound and plunging him into depression for the last two days of the retreat. As usual, I felt helpless to relieve his suffering, and could only try to stay close and weather the storm with him. In one of my talks I had referred to the scripture passage that proclaims "God is close to the broken-hearted." I knew that Byron would find little comfort in those words, and that it was up to me to be that "divine closeness." God, after all, does not play crib, at least as far as I know.

Both of us received many exuberant expressions of thanks as the retreat came to an end, but we were just eager to get into Claire's car and head for Paris. The clouds began to clear as we drove out of Brittany, and so, too, did Byron's depression. On the way we stopped at the great Gothic cathedral of Chartres. I was so keen for Byron to visit this magnificent edifice, and so thrilled to be sharing it with him, that I have no idea what he experienced as we walked under those soaring arches and gazed up at the intricate stained glass windows. I did observe how wide-eyed and enthusiastic he was seeing the Eiffel Tower, the Arc de Triomphe, the Champs Elysées, and other views of Paris by night as Claire drove us around on our way to Namaste, one of the l'Arche homes there in the city. He began repeating the line from the Second World War song "How ya gonna keep 'em down on the farm after they've seen *Paris*."

We were welcomed with great kindness and served a fine supper when we finally arrived at Namaste about 10 p.m. The next day, with our friend Ted Hyland, who was studying in Paris, we went to mass at Notre Dame Cathedral and then relaxed at an open air café, imbibing along with the coffee the delicious, vibrant atmosphere of the Left Bank. For Byron this was all new and exciting, and for me a flood of rich memories. I had lived for a year in Paris during my doctoral studies, and continued to come into the city regularly for the two years that I lived in Trosly. In the evening while Byron rested, I did some more memory-lane walking in the Jardin de Luxembourg, Montmartre, and other treasured areas of the city.

The next morning a friend, Jan Rissie, the founder of l'Arche in Mobile, Alabama, came by for breakfast and to drive us to the airport for our flight to Barcelona, Spain. Jan, who at the time was visiting the community in Paris, was far from comfortable driving in that busy city. It was not long before I found myself praying fervently to my good friend St. Martin de Porres to get us safely to the airport. Two minutes later, in a moment of uncertainty about directions, Jan slammed on the brakes, causing the woman in the car behind to run into us. No damage was done to our car, but we had to follow this woman to her nearby place of work to get papers for her insurance claim. The two hours that Jan had estimated for our trip to the airport was fast being consumed, but I tried my best not to lose faith in my friend St. Martin, who to that point had never let me down. Not wanting to make our driver any more flustered, I asked in as calm a tone as I could, "Jan, do we have far to go to get to Orly?"

"Orly?" she replied. "I thought you were flying from Roissy. I was heading for the wrong airport. Actually, Orly is quite close. We'll be there in no time." I smiled and said a silent prayer of thanks to Martin de Porres, who had come through again — albeit at the cost of a crumpled front bumper and grille.

After a 90-minute flight, we were in Barcelona, where we were met and driven to the little l'Arche community in the village of Moia, another 90 minutes through the mountains on a brilliantly sunny afternoon. The bright sun, however, was deceptive. We were shocked at how cold it was when we stepped out of the car and how much colder still when we stepped inside the quaint two-storey dwelling that was home to the eight-member household. It was not long before Byron was stuffing wood into the little stove in the living room and, later on, into a similar stove on the second floor, where the bedrooms were situated. The folks there probably had never known those stoves to get so hot, but still the two of us were only comfortable when we were huddled near one of these stoves. It helped considerably that the people in the home were extremely warm and welcoming.

During our stay in Moia, someone drove us to visit the nearby Jesuit landmarks of Manresa and Monserrat. This trip was a wonderful surprise for me. I was thrilled to be able to tap into the wellspring of my Jesuit vocation. It was in the town of Manresa that St. Ignatius of Loyola, the founder of the Jesuits, spent almost a year deepening his conversion experience from soldier of a temporal king to soldier of the Eternal King, living the prayer experiences that he distilled into his little handbook known as The Spiritual Exercises. These Spiritual Exercises are what have shaped the spirituality of every Jesuit, from the first companions that Ignatius gathered around him at the University of Paris in the early 1500s to the over 20,000 Jesuits around the world today.

A huge stone edifice has been built over the little cave where, as a pilgrim, Ignatius lived and prayed in extreme austerity. The Jesuits now operate it as a centre of prayer and spiritual renewal.

On this particular visit I could not help but remember my first pilgrimage to this hallowed shrine in the winter of 1967 during my final year of Jesuit formation, which I was doing in another part of Spain. The evening of my arrival, the Jesuit who was responsible for the building graciously welcomed me. When I eagerly asked if I could visit the cave, he said, "You will have plenty of time tomorrow to see the cave, but come, let me show you the new furnace I've just installed." Now, having spent the past two days in the nearby l'Arche home with Byron huddled around the wood stove, I was finally able to appreciate why that new furnace had been treated with such reverence. It also helped me to appreciate a little more what it would have been like for Ignatius to live through the freezing winter months in that hollow in the rocks.

Ignatius had come to Manresa from the ancient and well-known shrine of Monserrat, where he had spent several weeks in prayer. It was here that he ritualized his conversion from soldier to pilgrim by making an all-night vigil of arms, kneeling before the central altar on which was enshrined the statue of Our Lady of Monserrat, commonly known as the Black Madonna. This visit brought back memories of a day of prayer and reflection that our total community – the Farm Community along with Jesuit community and staff in Guelph – had lived a few years earlier. At one point during that day, the participants had been divided into groups of five or six. Each group was asked to mime a particular episode from the life of St. Ignatius. This Monserrat episode was the one chosen for our group, and guess who was the Black Madonna? It may have been my greatest performance, but I'm afraid the others were moved more to laughter than to devotion.

I was deeply moved to be revisiting these historic Jesuit sites, but Byron was more impressed by the dramatic, mountainous landscape in which they were set. While visiting these places, his overriding concern was how soon he could get outside to have a cigarette. However, being there with him, I was sensing an affinity between him and Ignatius, a parallel between his life and that of the founder of the Jesuits. Ignatius' life journey was radically altered when a cannonball shattered his leg. During his time of convalescence he felt called to do heroic deeds for God rather than for his king and the princess of his dreams, a conversion from ferocious soldier and *bon vivant* into a saint and mystic. Byron's life, on the other hand, was radically changed by the bullet that shattered his face. He did not have the dramatic religious conversion of Ignatius, but gradually he was being transformed into a gentler man, heroically struggling to overcome his anger and addictions and through this struggle becoming a man of compassion. Byron was no saint, at least not by any traditional understanding of that term, but being with him in these places was helping me to appreciate the nobility of his ongoing struggle to reclaim his life from the ashes of the past, all of which was helping me to appreciate the person and life of my spiritual father, St. Ignatius of Loyola.

After a few days in Moia we left the mountains to visit the other l'Arche community, El Rusc, closer to Barcelona but out in the countryside. Several of the residents had been living here for many years and were older and more settled. Byron seemed to relax and feel more settled as well. He was able to connect with these people extremely well, sharing cigarettes with them, teasing them and getting them to laugh with him, all with non-verbal communication. He was relating to the people better than I was, even though I was the one who could speak Spanish. While I was struggling to understand their words, he was simply enjoying heart-to-heart communion.

Then, on the weekend, we gathered at a retreat centre in the city with most of the members of the two communities along with a number of their friends and associates. I gave the opening talk on Friday evening, and was to give two more talks on Saturday and a concluding talk on Sunday morning. However, during the night I became very ill with vomiting and diarrhea, so that by morning I was too weak to get out of bed. The retreat had to proceed without me. A doctor who was participating in the weekend came to see me and was able to assure me that I was not dying. In fact, she was more concerned about Byron's severe coughing, and put him on antibiotics. By the evening, thanks to the medication she had given me, I was able to eat a little rice and dry toast. Several people came to visit me during the day but the most consoling visits were with Byron. He made me laugh with his version of how the retreat was proceeding. He was not picking up on any of the content, but his descriptions of some of the participants, especially those taking my place, were priceless. He also told me with great delight about his conversation with Alejandra, one of the women from El Rusc: "We sat together under a tree and talked and talked for over an hour. I didn't understand a word she was saying and she didn't understand me but we had such a good conversation. It was wonderful."

I was touched when he came again in the evening, perhaps his fourth visit of the day, saying apologetically, "I had to come. I couldn't stay away, I missed you so much."

By Sunday morning I was well enough to participate in the closing liturgy. We all held hands as we prayed the Our Father, followed by a prayer for peace. During this prayer there was a smile on Byron's face the likes of which I had rarely seen. I was a bit non-plussed at the copious and effusive expressions of gratitude that were lavished on us at the end, since I had contributed so little to the weekend experience. However, it delighted me that the accolades were for both Byron and me without any distinction.

The retreatants all left by early afternoon, and then Byron and I were taken on a tour of the city. This was enjoyable enough, but I was relieved when our guides brought us back to the empty retreat centre where we could spend a quiet evening alone.

That night I dreamed that I was in the front passenger seat of a van full of people from l'Arche. When the van stopped to let out a number of them, Barbara, the first person I had met on my arrival at l'Arche in 1968, lovingly handed me a tiny woman whose face was badly scarred and bruised from recent surgery. Looking into the face of this fragile, wounded figure I was moved with deep love. Holding her tenderly in my arms I stepped out of the van to bid farewell to those who were leaving. I turned and saw the van leaving without me. With this precious treasure in my arms, I began to run after it. Fortunately, the driver caught sight of us in his rear-view mirror and came back for us. Then I was in a home resting next to this little woman, who seemed to get lost in the covers. When she emerged, to my amazement, she was speaking and speaking in English, and her face was flawless, rosy and bright like that of a little child. When I woke I wondered to whom that transformed face belonged: to Byron or my own inner child or my mother or whomever. I felt a deep peace, sensing that thanks to these past couple of weeks I had come to a new level of integration and communion with the people and communities that were a part of my life and with myself.

In the morning we were on the train from Barcelona to Madrid, where we would visit a dear Jesuit friend of mine before heading back to Canada. I had feared that the eight-hour trip would be boring, but it turned out to be quite the contrary. En route we played a few games of crib, but mostly we just stared out the windows of the train and drank in the fascinating scenery. At first we saw the rugged coastline, which occasionally gave way to stretches of beautiful beaches bordering the deep blue waters of the Mediterranean. Then, at Tarragona, we headed inland through the mountains and across the great central plateau to Zaragoza and down to Madrid. We saw farmland that differed completely from that of southern Ontario: vast stretches of sun-baked and parched land that somehow was nourishing patches of cornfields, vineyards and olive groves. In places, the houses of baked clay seemed to be natural outcrops of the earth itself, and the people around them just as rooted in the soil as the gardens and orchards they were tending. Then, dramatically, all this changed as we approached Madrid and began passing miles and miles of high-rise apartments densely crowded together.

My friend Patin (pronounced Pateen, a nickname for Valentin) met us at the station and took us by taxi to our hostel in the heart of the old city, which in this early evening was pulsating with life. He was very apologetic that his own Jesuit community was not open to welcoming lay people to stay with them, knowing as he did that this would not have been the case in Canada. I assured him that this was not a problem and that Byron and I were quite content with the lodging he had found for us. We were sharing a fairly spacious room in this modest residence where our hostess, Katti, a kind, motherly type, did all she could to make us feel welcome. While Byron sipped on the *café con leche* that Katti brought to him, Patin and I went out in search of food to bring back for our supper.

By the next day Byron was all choked up with the cold in his head and chest and was depressed, as often happened when he took antibiotics, so he could hardly share my enthusiasm about being in Madrid. Fortunately, he was getting engrossed in the book *Papillon*, the autobiography of an escaped convict that he had picked up at the Shakespeare and Company bookstore on the Left Bank in Paris. He was content to spend much of the day resting, reading and drinking the *café con leche* that Katti would supply on demand. The one gentle afternoon stroll through the city with me and Patin, who had a brilliant knowledge of the city and a delightful sense of humour, did manage to lift Byron's spirits. A bullfight would have done more for him, perhaps, but this was not the season.

I was pleased to be renewing my friendship with Patin, and especially happy for the few times that the three of us were together either on a walk or visiting in the hostel. Byron and Patin related easily together, enjoying each other's humour. My time alone with Byron had a special quality of tenderness: the meals that I brought in for us, the crib games, the daily mass, the late-night conversations when both of us were having trouble sleeping. Perhaps this was due in part to his frailty and my concern for his health, but it was also due to the deeper level of companionship that we had reached through all that we had shared together on this trip. I missed him when I went alone to see again the works of the great masters El Greco, Velasquez and Goya in the Prado art gallery, and when I went with Patin once for a meal at the Jesuit residence and once to a restaurant.

It was on our last evening in Madrid that Patin and I went to Hemingway's favourite restaurant, where I ate the traditional bread soup and pork roasted in a wood-burning oven, accompanied of course by a bottle of strong red wine. From there we walked back to the hostel to find Byron contentedly sitting up in bed reading *Papillon*. After the farewells I quickly packed for the two of us as Byron continued to read. Then we took time to say a prayer of thanksgiving for all that we had lived during this amazing trip. Moments later I looked over at Byron, already asleep in the opposite bed, and felt content; tomorrow night we would be in our own beds in the Farm House. As I continued to watch him sleep and listen to him snore, it struck me that here was a personality every bit as extraordinary as any of Hemingway's characters or as the renowned author himself. Many could enjoy the privilege of eating in Ernest Hemingway's favourite restaurant, but I had the privilege, however dubious at times, of sharing a room with Byron Dunn.

★ ★ ★ ★ ★

MEANWHILE, BACK AT THE RANCH

Dear Mum and Dad,

I'm sitting at the table and Ruthanne and Byron are playing tootsies (footsies but more discreet). Byron got drunk and went to a motel and at one point fell over and broke several ribs. So he's quite sore and can't sleep. Ruthanne has been here for a week and we've been having a fabulous time. I've been dressing her, undressing her and bathing her. She can make me laugh so much that I can just think of something she said or did for the rest of the day and start laughing all over again. Poor Byron, it hurts him to laugh or cough, both of which he normally does most of the day long.

Another friend of Bill's has been staying – Josianne from France. It's funny watching Bill try to juggle the three of them: Ruthanne who's barely intelligible because of her cerebral palsy, Byron who has no tongue and so is difficult to understand at the best of times but now is even worse because he's just got some new teeth, and Josianne who doesn't speak any English at all. Update: Ruthanne has just clawed off Byron's shoe in an attempt to seduce him and they are both laughing like drains, pain or no pain.

Love,
Weesa

14

God's Gifts Can Be Badly Wrapped

It took Byron and me some time to recover from jet lag once we returned from Spain, but otherwise life resumed as usual, except for one slight shift. The time together, the sharing with him of my ministry to l'Arche and many of my friends abroad, had taken our friendship to a deeper level. The result was that in our relationship the good times were better than ever but the conflicts and tensions were more delicate and more painful.

It wasn't long before he was drinking again, which came to a crisis one Monday morning when Sr. Christine was at the Farm House cooking lunch for the community. On the weekend Byron had gotten several bottles of wine as a way of coping with depression. When I came in from the farm to check on him, Christine stopped me in the kitchen to discuss the situation, which she rightly felt was becoming intolerable. While we were talking, Byron came out of the bedroom and through the kitchen. He was doing his best not to stagger but he was wobbling like a man trying to carry a huge burden that was more than he could manage. He glanced shamefully at us through blurry eyes and stumbled into the bathroom on the far side of the kitchen. Christine and I stared silently at each other and at the bathroom door in disgust as we listened to him violently throwing up. When he finally came out, looking very old and very sick with his eyes watering and mucus running from the holes in his face where a nose should be, Christine lit into him.

"Byron, this has got to stop and it has to stop now! You're making a fool of yourself and you're making fools of us. If you want to destroy your life, then go somewhere else and do it. You can't expect us to keep putting up with this craziness. When you look at what drinking has done to your life already, how can you think it could solve anything? You'd better smarten up and decide what you want to do because we can't put up with this any longer."

Byron, hanging onto a chair for support, stood with his mouth open and eyes bulging, taking in Christine's words almost gratefully, it seemed. He didn't say a word, but gazing at her with tears welling up in his glassy eyes, nodded his agreement. Then he turned that face full of misery towards me as he continued nodding as if begging to be scolded some more. I don't know if he could read in my eyes all that was there: fear, anger, frustration, disgust, discouragement and compassion.

A little later in the bedroom, after he had drunk more wine and slept, he suggested that I should be talking tough with him the way Christine had done, which stabbed me in a place of great vulnerability. It felt as though he was laying blame on me for his drinking. Byron was very dependent on me, but in some strange way I related to him as to a father. I also linked him to my mother and her 30-year struggle with alcohol, a link that certainly contributed to my inability to confront him more directly and sternly. In any case, at that moment I was too hurt and angry to respond, but was thinking, "You bastard, you've got your nerve comparing my way to Christine's, and what difference would it make anyway? You're going to keep on drinking yourself to death no matter what anyone says or does."

A large, icy hand closed tightly around my heart. I could not even look at him and was totally disinterested when he promised that from then on he would no longer drink in the house. He gave me his wallet and chequebook so he could not buy more booze. Later that day, I reluctantly accepted his invitation to play cribbage. As we played, the wall between us began to melt. Finally, he spoke. "I know that somehow I have to stop drinking, because if I don't it's going to destroy our friendship." I looked straight into his tearful, drooping eyes and nodded my agreement.

At the end of the day a few of us gathered in the chapel to celebrate mass. I was grateful when Byron came in to join us. During the time of intercessions he prayed, "God, please help me, give me the strength to stop drinking. Bless Bill and Christine and all those who have been putting up with me and trying to help me." At that moment I sensed a peace and a trust that his prayer would be answered and that our friendship would endure. But the answer was to be slow in coming, and in the meantime our friendship would be tested on more than one occasion.

That summer it was decided that I should replace Fr. Doug as the community leader. Since being named two years before this as the formation director for the Novices, young men aspiring to be Jesuits, Doug had been wearing the two leadership hats. At times he would be interrupted in an interview with one of his novices by a phone call from Bob announcing that they were out of milk at the Red House, or that the goats had gotten through the fence and were in the driveway and could end up on the highway. The Provincial Superior of the Jesuits was ready to name me as the new director of the Farm Community, so the community underwent a reflection process by which they affirmed me in this role.

At a community mass close to the official date, July 31, 1987, we celebrated a simple ritual of the transfer of authority. During the mass, Doug gave a homily about servant leadership after the example of Jesus, who washed the feet of his disciples as a concrete sign of Christian leadership: "I came not to be served but to serve and to lay down my life for my flock."

The image for our community was not that of a pyramid with the director at the peak and the more talented members just below, all the way down to the least significant ones at the base, but rather the circle in which we were simply friends, needing each other and relating to each other as equals. As much as possible we tried to share the leadership and responsibility. However, being Jesuit priests, Doug and I had a great deal of moral authority, and there were times when the community wanted to see our authority more strongly exercised. I remember Byron in a moment of frustration at all the chaos saying angrily, "I need to know who's in charge here." As the community leader, Doug had struggled to minimize his personal authority yet give the much-needed leadership that called everyone to take responsibility and prevent us from drowning in the chaos. I knew that this would be my challenge as well. What we both knew was that leadership was a role of humble service, not of honour or power.

As the service proceeded, Julie, back from her time in prison, reached up to put her hands on Doug's bowed head and prayed, "Dear God, thanks for Doug, he's a good man and I love him, he's been good to all of us and he always will be. Amen."

Mary the Russian Princess, putting her hands on my head, prayed, "God bless Bill and show him how to be a good director, and God bless all of us in the community because we're going to need it."

Mary, who loves me dearly, always has a way of coming up with the right phrase. One time the community was celebrating my birthday and someone was solemnly announcing that I had been born on July 20, 1932, to which Mary loudly proclaimed, "My Mom told me that was a bad year for ragweed."

After a good chuckle in response to Mary's prayer, we sang one of our favourites, the Shaker hymn "'Tis a Gift to Be Simple." Then I thanked Doug for his years of wise, generous leadership, and thanked the community members for their affirmation, asking for their continued prayers and support. I spoke of my own love and commitment to the community, but also of my conviction that Jesus loves and is committed to us as a community even more, and that he is the one who really holds us together and leads us.

In retrospect, perhaps I relied too much on Jesus to take care of things, and did not put enough of my own energy and time into the leadership challenge. I continued to travel as much as ever in my work with l'Arche. Now that I was director I was even more a source of security, so that my absences were felt more than before. I was convinced that the work with l'Arche was important, not just for l'Arche but for myself and the Farm Community, but I could understand the resentment that some would express about me flying all over the world to give talks about community while they had to stay home and live in the daily mess of it. If there was going to be a crisis in the community it would almost inevitably happen while I was away. Whoever met me at the airport as I returned from France or India or wherever, would have the task of briefing me on the various crises that had transpired and what kind of pieces I would have to pick up when I got home. It was always a pleasant surprise when all had gone smoothly during my absence, and would already be a great relief if I saw Byron among the welcoming party at the airport.

In late August of that year, Byron became more than usually depressed with all the comings and goings in the Farm House. Probably he was especially upset with the pending departure of Weesa, who had been very close to him during her three years with us. He started drinking and so, true to his word, left the house for a room at the local motel. He returned two days later still very shaky and with a bottle in his pickup truck to help him taper off. Weesa left the next day. While playing crib with him that evening I suggested that the two of us get away for a few days to the Jesuit rest house, a cottage in the nearby village of Belfountain. This cheered him immediately, and he was in good spirits for the entire week and a half of anticipation.

It was only when we got to Belfountain and began to relax that I realized that I needed the break as much as or more than he did. It was the second week of September and the trees had begun to put on their gold and red festive robes in this most beautiful area of Southern Ontario, at the forks of the Credit River. While enjoying the autumn beauty, we tried our luck fishing in various areas of the two branches of the river but, in Byron's words, "Our luck wasn't worth a pinch of coon shit." On our way back to Guelph, Byron insisted that we go to a fish hatchery where, for a fee, the public was allowed to fish in a special pond of mature trout. You were guaranteed to catch something. He just did not want to go back to the house empty-handed. He reminded me of his dad's motto: "Never go into a small town crying." This was the same phrase he quoted at me while I was losing badly to him at cribbage on the evening I assumed the leadership of the community, a motto that seemed to me the very antithesis of what the Farm Community was all about. Unfortunately, the hatchery turned out to be closed. However, even though we were skunked as far as the fishing was concerned, and Byron hated being skunked, we went home refreshed, not crying but laughing.

We also came home with a desire to do more fishing. So when our friend Dave invited us to go north to the Owen Sound area to fish for salmon, we jumped at the opportunity, even though it meant rising before four in the morning in order to get an early start. It was six o'clock the next morning when we returned – slightly delirious with aching, exhausted bodies and bleary, bloodshot eyes, and four 20- to 25-pound salmon. Somehow we managed to smile for the camera with the delayed shutter action that I set up on the edge of the woodbox to capture the two of us holding up the proof of our expertise as fishermen. Then Byron immediately collapsed into bed while I spent the next hour and a half cleaning the huge fish and then cleaning the mess in the kitchen before Sr. Liz came down.

It would be a violation of the fishermen's code to tell the entire true story of all that transpired during that 26-hour expedition. I can say that we had almost reached the point of total frustration and fatigue before Byron finally hooked and landed our first fish. Before that the three of us were standing along the river bank fishing in vain with our sophisticated gear when a scrawny 12-year-old with a cheap little rod and reel walked by. Twenty minutes later he came back dragging a fish that was almost as big as himself, saying to us as he passed, "This sure is heavy." He was too innocent to have any idea how close he was to being thrown into the river along with his cheap little rod and big heavy fish. Before we left for home, Dave's friend Jimmy, a great fisherman who lives in the area, threw a fish to me, saying, "Here, catch! Now if anyone asks, you can say you *caught* it." So the truth is, we did catch a hundred pounds of salmon, one way or another.

Christmas as always was a difficult time for Byron, but he seemed to manage this one better than most, even coming with us to midnight mass with the extended community at Ignatius College. After a simple *réveillon* celebration following the mass, our household came back home to open gifts. Byron was able to sit with us for a short while in the living room by the Christmas tree. He wanted to see me open the gift he had got me and wrapped in my old work jacket. This was consistent with an expression he would use on many different occasions, whether to embellish or wrap or hide something or protect or keep something warm: "Throw an old coat over it." He chuckled watching me struggle to undo the abundant binder twine "ribbons" to discover a new tool box inside the smelly jacket.

Five hours later, at 8 a.m., Liz and I were up stuffing the 25-pound turkey and getting it into the oven. This was one of the smaller turkeys we had raised on the farm that year. Then at 10 a.m., accompanied by Val with her guitar and Weesa, who was visiting, I went to the Correctional Centre to celebrate mass for a handful of inmates. Since Byron and other community members over the years had come from this Centre, I was always ready and willing to go there for special occasions. That evening, Byron actually came with us to the other house for the community dinner, using one of the bedrooms there as his dining room. It seems that he was too shaky to stay home alone and wait for me to bring his meal.

The next day I was away from the house visiting family and friends until late in the evening. It was a relief to find Byron home and in bed when I got in. For the next couple of days I was on with a small team to do the morning and afternoon barn chores, and in between these I played a number of crib games with Byron and generally tried to be present to him. It seemed that he was getting through this difficult season better than in previous years.

One of these nights I had a very vivid dream about my own death. I was in a Jesuit residence like Ignatius College. I had a terminal illness that was causing some pain in my chest, obstructing my breathing and making me very weak. Fr. Monaghan, who had been the superior when I was a novice at Ignatius, was attending to me as I was close to death. He was leaning towards me kindly in his food-stained black cassock, his round rimless glasses sliding down his nose, the tufts of white hair framing his balding head. I asked him to tell my mother that I was sorry to be dying before her and to thank her for having been a perfect mother. I was feeling some slight sadness but mostly peace and deep gratitude. Then, about to enter the elevator with some other Jesuits, I swooned, shook hands with a couple of friends and died. Somehow I was observing my own dead body from above. One leg was twitching and I was worried that people might doubt that I was dead. Then my whole body was twitching, at which point I awoke. The peace and gratitude that filled me during the dream continued for some time afterward. Something in me was dying to allow new life to rise up, but I was not sure exactly what. I suspect that it had something to do with an earlier dream, indicating that a kind of "religiosity" in me needed to continue dying to give way to a more authentic and personal way of being. Although Byron was not in the dream explicitly, I sensed that our relationship was at play in it. Certainly, in my relationship with him as well as with others in the community I was being called to be simply a friend, a brother and at times a father, but not *Father*, someone special on a pedestal. I was becoming more aware that being a priest and a Jesuit was simply a way of being the human person that God, through the community, was calling me to be. Whether celebrating mass, leading a council meeting, shovelling manure, cooking a meal or playing crib I was totally Jesuit priest, and totally and only this poor human being, with my various gifts and numerous shortcomings.

Central to that dream about my death was the deep gratitude I had for my mother, and my apology for dying ahead of her. In real life I was experiencing a deepening appreciation and thankfulness for Mom. She was aging so gracefully, becoming more peaceful and faith-filled.

In the same way I was also growing in appreciation for all my family: my sister and brothers and their children. It could be that, years earlier when I made the choice to join the Jesuits, there was some great longing for a permanent family. At the time of that decision my brothers and sister were already married, or at the point of being so. My happiest childhood memories are those of being together with them, such as when the four of us would walk the couple of blocks to the top of our street in Oakville and wait for the bus that would be bringing Dad home from Toronto after his five-day rail trip to Winnipeg or twice that to Vancouver. Being the youngest I always sensed it as a great privilege when I was included with the others. There were enough times when they made it clear that they didn't want me around, especially Rob and Gord. There were things they wanted to do that were better done without their baby brother who had a need to tell everything to Mom. So it could have been that later, as they were choosing their spouses, I had the feeling that they were again going off and leaving their kid brother behind, but this time in a more permanent way. I would have to find my own family.

At that point in my life there was no attraction to having my own wife and children. My shyness made dating a daunting challenge even though I was strongly attracted to girls and longed for an intimate, steady relationship. It was only in the six months prior to being accepted by the Jesuits that I had started to develop a somewhat serious relationship with a girlfriend. I had gotten beyond my shyness and was very much enjoying her company. Although it cost me some effort to relinquish the relationship, I only realized later, from my brother Gord who had introduced us, that it had been a suffering for her as well. I still feel ashamed of the fact that I only communicated to her by letter my decision for a celibate life.

The day I actually left home for Guelph to join the Jesuits was one of the most difficult of my life to that point. Saying goodbye to Mom and Dad, and then to Rob and his family, and finally to my sister Betty and her family seemed like a definitive farewell. Gord, who hated goodbyes, simply disappeared to avoid having to see me off. I was, it seemed, giving up my own flesh-and-blood family in favour of religious community, which might or might not prove to be a kind of spiritual family. In those days, such a departure was in fact a radical letting go of family. During my three years at Guelph I had only two or three visits from my parents – I don't recall any from my siblings – and I could make no visits to them. After that I went off to Spokane, Washington, for three years of philosophy studies. I had a short visit home on my way from Spokane to Halifax, where I taught at the Jesuit St. Mary's University and High School. It was during that year that Dad died suddenly of a heart attack. I went home for the funeral but stayed just a couple of days. The next year I returned to Toronto, where I spent four years studying theology, being ordained to the priesthood at the end of the third year. During this time I began to reconnect with family and was very grateful to do so. Perhaps that definitive separation imposed at the beginning of the formation was intended to foster a stronger sense of belonging with my Jesuit family, and perhaps it did. However, they are two different levels or degrees of belonging that I now experience as complementing rather than competing with each other: both are very important.

I lived community life in the Jesuits with a reasonable amount of contentment, but it was certainly not family life as I had known it. In the first years of Jesuit formation, "particular friendships" were frowned upon – in fact, we were even discouraged from calling one another by our first names. Officially, I was Brother Clarke, or simply Brother or Bro, but never just plain Bill. Of course, the rule was one thing, and how we lived it quite another. We did know and call one another by first names and gradually developed friendships, at least with some. Over the years I have developed deep and lasting friendships with Jesuits as well as with other men and women, all of which have strengthened my sense of belonging within the Jesuit family and in the larger family of the Church.

Before joining the Jesuits I had only a vague sense of being part of the body or family of the Church. Other than Sunday mass, my family had almost no involvement with the social life of the parish, both in Oakville and later Toronto. In both places, with a few rare exceptions, I was unaware of any of my friends being practising Roman Catholics. It was when I joined the boxing team during my second year at university that I had my first experience of socializing with a group of Catholics and experiencing my faith as something other than merely a private affair between me and God.

I had taken up boxing just to get some healthy exercise, after being convinced by my sister not to continue playing football, as I had done in my first year with the engineers in the inter-faculty league. Betty felt that with this rough sport of football I was risking an injury that could be detrimental to my studies. As it turned out, the boxing coach, Tony Canzano, and the majority of the boxing team were Catholics. Our end of the season party, a major event, was always held on March 17, since we considered that St. Patrick's Day gave us an exemption from the Lenten discipline. This experience of belonging in the Church with other Catholics probably contributed to my openness to religious community.

When I returned to Toronto for theology studies and reconnected with my own family, I began to realize that I felt there a belonging that is fundamentally important for my identity. That my mother has known and loved me from the time of my conception is an immeasurable gift. There is much about my adult life of which my mom and siblings have little or no awareness, just as there is so much of their lives about which I know nothing, but in a very deep place we have always known each other with knowledge of the heart. When they call me by name I hear it as I've heard it from my earliest childhood, which tells me who I am in a very radical way. There are, necessarily and fortunately, limitations to this particular belonging. I am and will always be Louis and Jessie's son and the younger brother of Rob, Betty and Gord. The positive aspects as well as all that has been lacking in this family unit have gone a long way towards shaping who I am today, helping me to trust in the possibility of other relationships and different forms of family or community as well as revealing my longing for more. One's own family, however wonderful it might be, can never be enough.

The most significant limitation within our family of which I was conscious was the lack of affection and affirmation from my dad. He was a good and generous man who worked hard to provide for us, but his work took him away a great deal and he was not very free or expressive with the affection I'm sure he had for me and my siblings. His desire for us to achieve academically made him tend always to urge us to do better rather than affirm what we did achieve. Since my brother Gord was most like Dad in personality, I and all of us in later years longed for his affection and affirmation in a similar way as we had done with Dad. I suppose my love for Gord and my need for his affection influenced my relationship with Byron. I would say that with Gord, as brothers we gradually became friends, and with Byron, as friends we gradually became brothers, the latter relationship being fraught with much more struggle than the former. This very struggle in my journey with Byron was teaching me a great deal about the preciousness of friendship and brotherhood; neither could be taken for granted.

I was shocked and frightened a couple of years ago when Gord was diagnosed with lung cancer, but thanks to all that I had lived with Byron I was able to be more present to him in his final journey and to deeply grieve his passing. Byron and the Farm Community were causing me to lose some of my ability to deny pain, helping me to be more human.

So, as it turned out, it was Gord and not me who died while Mom was still alive. This was a terrible blow to her, but she was able to handle the pain by calling upon the resource of her deep faith and her close friendship with St. Joseph on whose feast day, March 19, she was born. A few hours after she had learned of Gord's death she received a phone call in the nursing home where she lived from her closest grandchild, Elizabeth, who wanted to offer some comfort. Mom said apologetically, "I'm sorry, Liz, I can't talk to you right now. I'm talking to St. Joseph – he's holding my hand." I'm sure it was this intimate relationship with St. Joseph that had helped her overcome her drinking problem.

The next challenge for Byron and me was New Year's. On New Year's Eve I stayed home with him while most of our household went to the Red House for a little party. Christine came for an hour to visit and play crib with us. By about 10 p.m. Byron and I were alone in the bedroom where we sat on our beds and talked a little, but mostly he just cried. We went to the kitchen for a coffee because the room felt too depressing.

"I wish I could pray," he said, "but I'm too angry with God."

I encouraged him to let God have it. "God can handle your anger, Pal, and telling God how angry you are is good prayer."

He talked about some of the New Year's he had lived with his family. He may never have been sober for any of them, but I sensed that there had been meaningful relationships, even if they were experienced while racing through the night on snowmobiles. By the time midnight struck, he was in bed asleep and I was in the chapel giving thanks for the year and praying that the coming year would be blessed for all of us, especially Byron. I added, as I often did, the special intention that he not die a violent death, confiding him to the care of St. Joseph, the patron saint of a happy death, and after whom Byron had received his middle name.

On New Year's morning, according to our tradition, the community, accompanied by numerous friends, celebrated mass in the barn. We huddled together to keep from freezing, grateful for the warmth of the cattle and manure, if not for the smell, and for the way some of the cows would stretch their heads through the manger to eat the bales of hay out from under those who were sitting on them just a little too close to the pen. This celebration always seemed to give me courage, helping me realize how the God who came to us as the tiny infant in the humble stable of Bethlehem continues to be manifested in the littleness and messiness of our daily lives.

A few days later Byron was out in the afternoon and when he returned he told me he had two bottles of wine and a bottle of whisky. During the night he had dreamed of having a peaceful conversation with his wife, and he woke up crying. I challenged him about the hopelessness of his drinking and how he was destroying his life and risking an accident or some other form of violence. I tried to make him see the futility and the danger of this behaviour, and how he owed it to himself and to his family to end the destructive pattern; he had already inflicted more than enough pain on them and on himself. He acknowledged the truth of what I was saying but he was stuck. He had to have a drink and he knew that he should not be drinking in the house, but he clearly dreaded going to the motel. We ended with a compromise. He handed over the whisky and agreed to go slowly with the wine. I doubted the wisdom of allowing him to drink in the house but I did not have the heart to send him out.

In the middle of May I went as usual to the hermitage for my annual eight-day retreat. I felt badly about leaving Byron and the others, but I desperately needed this time of solitude and prayer in the quiet of this little cabin set in an isolated and beautiful area of the farm. Byron drove me out there on the first day with food supplies and enough water for three or four days. I would be able to walk to the barn for more fresh water when my supply ran out. Byron hugged me rather desperately before getting back into his truck to leave.

"I'll be praying for you, Pal," I told him as encouragingly as I could.

"You better, 'cause I'm going to need it."

By the afternoon of day two I was beginning to unwind and bask in the deep, comforting stillness. Suddenly I was startled by a knock at the door. My heart sank when Byron came in looking at me apologetically. I did my best to hide my resentment for the intrusion, and tried to show him hospitality. He was probably too desperate to pick up on my negative reaction to this invasion of my precious privacy. By the time he finished sipping the coffee I made him, I was feeling more accepting of his presence and asked if he would like to celebrate mass with me. He was delighted, and during the mass I felt a deep sense of gratitude for his companionship and for the privilege of having him pray with me. For the rest of the retreat I eagerly looked for him to come each day for mass. The one rainy day when he didn't come because it was too wet to drive up the hill I missed him terribly. Rather than being a distraction from my prayer and solitude, it seemed that Byron had been sent to support me and to help keep my prayer grounded and real.

One night during this retreat I had another vivid dream in which I experienced some very life-giving camaraderie with a group of engineering classmates (some of whom I continue to meet periodically at class reunions), and also but to a lesser extent with a group of Jesuit novices. In the prayer that followed the dream I became aware of a heaviness in me. I realized that during the past year I had not laughed very much, nor had I initiated much that could bring joy to others. I noticed that my spirit had been sinking into passivity and sadness. Gradually it dawned on me that part of the problem had been my failure to adequately grieve the many losses of recent years, especially the numerous departures of community members. These departures had affected me directly as well as through the pain they had caused in Byron. Now I was being invited to overcome my passivity by choosing life and choosing joy, and to give thanks – not just for the obvious blessings but for everything.

Like Byron's Christmas gift wrapped in my stinky old barn jacket and binder twine, God's gifts sometimes come badly wrapped: disappointment, hurt, loss, loneliness, and so on. Thanksgiving, I realized, is what is required to unwrap these seemingly unappealing gifts and discover the hidden treasure within. As I began to give thanks and to actively grieve past hurts and let go of friends who had left, I was able to more gratefully welcome those who had recently arrived and accept them for who they are and accept the community in its present form. This process also helped me to welcome Byron more completely as he is today and let go of some of my fear about what might happen to him with his declining health and ongoing struggle with addictions. These themes of grieving and giving thanks were not new to me, but they were a timely reminder of the Jesuit way of finding God in all things. It was clear that I still had a long way to go, but at least the desire was there to be more wholly present to all that I'm given to live in the concrete unfolding of my days, months and years. It was important at that time to claim the truth that the Farm Community is my place of belonging, my home, and that for better or for worse Byron and I and the other members of the community have been given to each other as brothers and sisters.

MEANWHILE, BACK AT THE RANCH

Dear Mum and Dad,

It's a hot night and I've been working until dark and I'm exhausted but too wound up to sleep. Paul has been away and Pat O'Connor has left the farm so I've been in charge, and it's haymaking time so I have to make these terrible decisions. Shall I rake? Will it rain? Shall I bale now? Shall I cut some more hay? The weather has been very strange, hot and humid and sudden thunderstorms, making it hard to bring in hay. There's also a workforce of 15 to find work for, try to match people who won't fight or destroy machinery, etc. I'm not good at it, I'm anxious all the time, so I get a bit bossy. We were building fences, haymaking, herding and separating cattle and fixing equipment all week.

Fortunately a lot of the visitors at the farm this summer want to prove their manhood to one another quite desperately. This means I can relax and do other things while they flex their muscles at each other as they fling the bales up into the haymow. Machismo has its place on a farm at haying time.

Then tonight I was baling, it was a beautiful sunset, and a beautiful field, and across the hill was a swarm of people gathering bales, and the baler was working fine for a while, and I felt at peace and in love with God and world, and suddenly I saw some people running fast across the field towards the full wagon, and when I came around the corner I saw they'd lost the whole wagonload. The bales were lying in a chaotic mountain on the ground, and I knew there had been people sitting on top of that load, and I thought, they must be all underneath lying with broken limbs or suffocated. The bales were all damp and heavy, too. There had been five people on top and they all fell, and it's a long way down. Miraculously, no one was hurt. Another miracle. We have some mighty active guardian angels around here, with the particular combination of people and machinery that we are working with.

Love from

Weesa

15

Never Go into a Small Town Crying

The seasons flowed by with their rhythms of work and worship and play, of fruitfulness and fallow time. The pruning of the orchard continued into the early spring, along with the tapping of the sugar maples and the enjoyable but time-consuming work of collecting the sap and the 40:1 boiling down into sweet, dark syrup. Then came the working of the fields and the seeding of grain and corn accompanied by the usual picking of rocks (a tedious job made pleasant by the fact that everyone could participate and it had to be done together). Some fields, thanks to the winter frost, yielded a rich harvest of rocks every spring. During or just after the time of the apple blossoms we would celebrate the blessing of the land. Throughout this time there would be the late-night barn checks until the last of the spring calves, lambs and kids were born. Next came the more meticulous work of planting the vegetable gardens. We all shared in the exuberance of the cavorting cattle when they were let out of the barnyards into the fresh pastures.

By late spring and early summer we were already busy bringing in the first cut of hay: work that treated us to scratched arms, sore muscles, eyes tired and bloodshot from the dust, holes in the knees of our jeans, a feeling of well-being along with fatigue as we worked ourselves into shape, and finally a great sense of accomplishment as we watched the two barns filling towards the rafters. Usually we would go on some kind of fun outing or have a party to celebrate the completion of the first cut of hay and then do it again at the end of the second cut. Summer also included many visitors and volunteers who joined us in tending the gardens and harvesting, canning and freezing fruits and vegetables. This work, along with the picking of the apples, continued into the fall. Sometimes there would also be maintenance work to do on our two homes: painting, repairs, the cleaning of stoves and chimneys and so forth, but always just the bare minimum because of our tight budget and the constant demands of the farm. Only one or two people had the expertise to run the combine for the grain harvest, but most of us could share in baling and bringing in the straw – work that seemed amazingly easy after having handled 10- to 15,000 bales of the much heavier hay.

Usually in the fall there would be a batch of some 40 meat chickens to slaughter, pluck, clean and pack into freezers. Thanksgiving Day was one of our most important celebrations as it combined acknowledging the birthday of the community as well as the blessings of the harvest. Once the apple picking was finished in November, it was time to begin the ongoing work of sorting and pressing some of them into cider, and pruning the trees. When the cattle were brought in from the pastures the fall calving may or may not have finished, but the slower-paced winter routines would set in, focused on the daily barn chores of feeding and bedding the livestock.

Work in the bush, mainly done in the fall, included cutting cedars for fence posts, and dead hardwood trees for firewood. Sawing these into logs, then splitting and stacking them, was work that continued sporadically throughout the winter months into the spring. Building and repairing equipment, barns, sheds, hay wagons, fences and so forth, was ongoing as the need arose and the weather allowed. Throughout the long winter months the haylofts gradually dwindled while the calves grew and the steers got heavy and the cows filled out with the swelling life within them.

Of course, not all of the hay and grain we fed into the livestock converted into animal flesh. Daily the manure got deeper and kept us shovelling and forking, fortunately with the aid of the front-end loader on the tractor. Finally, the spring calving would start and the cycle would begin again.

Against this background of the seasons and cycles of work, our life together in community unfolded. Gradually, almost imperceptibly, Byron began to get some control over his addiction to alcohol. It was only much later that I realized that his and my prayer for this victory was being answered. Meanwhile, there were still some very difficult moments.

One evening I came into the room to find him lying on his bed with blood oozing from a great gash in his forehead. In his drunkenness he had fallen in the kitchen and struck his head on the corner of the cast iron stove. There being no one home at the time, he had managed to crawl back to the bedroom leaving a trail of blood, which I only noticed afterwards. It was a challenge to get him on his feet, in and out of the car and then to the reception at the General Hospital emergency department. The way I was staggering, with his arm and much of his weight draped over my shoulder, it probably looked to the crowd in the waiting room like we were both drunk. As usual he did not have to wait long to see a doctor. He once explained to me that his secret at the emergency reception was never to look into the nurse's eyes and to look as much as possible like he was at death's door. It seemed to me that he did not have to do an Academy Award performance to achieve this effect.

The nurse and doctor were happy to have me accompany Byron into a cubicle so that I could help translate the conversation. By this time Byron was getting sober enough to have his sense of humour kick in. In answer to their question about what had happened, he explained very grimly how I had hit him with an axe. So the doctor asked if that is also the way he lost his nose. "No, a bear bit that off," he told them. It took 10 stitches to close the wound. This time I resisted the temptation to give him another angry but futile lecture.

On another occasion Byron was badly depressed for a couple of weeks. His doctor put him on a different antidepressant but it was not yet having any effect. Early one morning he asked me to take him to Emergency. I did so reluctantly, since I did not see how the hospital could help. I left him there and returned to the community for the weekly council meeting. When I called the hospital later to check on him I was surprised to discover that he had been admitted with a serious kidney infection, news that I received with mixed feelings. I was sorry that he was so sick but relieved that there was a physical explanation for the terrible state he had been in, about which something could be done. I also had a sense of relief that someone else would be taking care of him for the next few days. As it turned out he was in the hospital for over a week. By then I could hardly wait to have him home.

Byron was having fewer drinking episodes and was being asked by Christine to do more in support of the works she had created and was sustaining: the Welcome In drop-in centre, The Stepping Stone emergency shelter and the Dwelling Place, a longer-term shelter. Besides doing an increasing amount of driving to pick up and deliver food and used furniture, he was a supportive presence with Christine for the clientele of these various works for people in desperate need, spending time in the drop-in playing cards and chatting it up with the folks. This developing working relationship with Christine was bringing him to a greater sense of personal worth and independence from me and the Farm Community.

The emergency shelter was in the house that the Farm Community had built on our land, a house that had been occupied by the assistant farm manager and his family until their departure in 1987. This house had a basement apartment where Byron began spending the occasional weekend, which helped him test the possibility of a more independent life. Thus, when Christine began planning the creation of York Haven, a residence with individual bachelor apartments for disadvantaged people in need of semi-supported lodging, Byron was at least able to entertain this idea as a possibility for himself. At the same time I was reaching a level of independence that allowed me to imagine life in the Farm House without him. This new project of Christine's was still many months away from realization.

Unfortunately, the privacy of the basement apartment also gave Byron a place where he could drink without anyone bothering him. One evening as I was cleaning up the kitchen in the Farm House, he came staggering through the door. His 10 months of sobriety had ended, and I was shocked and upset to the point of speechlessness. I could only watch helplessly as he stumbled against the kitchen chairs and made his way to our room. Not long afterwards I heard him calling me. I rushed in to find him on the floor with his head split open. He had fallen and hit his head on the chair and couldn't get up. Taking in this scene, I exploded. "You stupid bastard!" I felt like picking up the chair and splitting his head even more. I was anything but gentle in helping him to his feet. When I said we had to go to Emergency, he stubbornly refused. Only when I calmed down enough to apologize did he agree to come with me. Watching him being led away by a nurse so that the doctor could put more stitches into that battle-scarred head of his, I began to feel some compassion stirring in my heart where before there had only been anger. While waiting, I stepped outside the hospital to be greeted by a magnificent sunset. Then I gave thanks.

The next morning there was no preventing him from getting in his truck to head for the North. I could only pray that he would be safe. It was a great relief when he called that night to say that he had made it okay and that there was no need to worry. I wasn't convinced, but that week we were very busy with the first cut of hay, so I had little time or energy left for worrying. He got back a week later from what he described as a terrible trip. He had met up with an old friend and drinking partner who was in worse condition than himself, and that seemed to shock him. Still drinking when he arrived home, he was very discouraged. Finally, I was able to convince him that all was not lost and that he just had to pick himself up and start again. The next day, with my encouragement, he went back to work with Christine.

Over the next few months, interspersed with a couple of enjoyable and relatively successful fishing trips, Byron had two or three more drinking bouts which included yet another trip to Emergency for even more stitches in his head. He could see that his body was becoming less able to handle the alcohol and that quitting was more than ever a matter of life or death.

During this time the community was going through a more than usually difficult period. As a result of interpersonal conflicts and perhaps my own inability as director to deal with these, several people became very disillusioned. The conflict began primarily as a mounting tension between two individuals with radically different personalities and very different expectations of community life. It seemed best for all concerned that one of them should leave — but which one? Some of the stronger personalities in the community took sides, while others disagreed with either the need for a decision or the process of coming to the decision. As a result, several people left. The fabric of the community seemed to be unravelling and it was no small challenge to prevent its total dissolution. When Byron was well it was a great source of peace and strength just to be able to sit with him in the evening and play crib and, without talking about the problems, feel his understanding and support. However, when he was not well it was almost more than I could handle. The community situation gradually began to resolve itself and return to some semblance of stability, but the stress of it probably contributed to Byron's awareness that he needed to live in a more stable environment. In a community like ours every departure, every new arrival affected everyone's life, to the point where it was almost a different community each time. Twelve years of living with this constant change was taking its toll on his fragile nervous system.

Meanwhile, Christine had opened York Haven and was inviting Byron to move there. York Haven was a project subsidized by the Ministry of Housing and Social Services to provide decent, affordable apartment-living in a supportive environment for people on welfare or disability pensions. Here, Byron would have the privacy of his own bachelor apartment as well as the companionship of others he could meet in the common room on his own terms if and when he chose to go there. More important, he would have the support of Christine, who was also living there and overseeing the care of the residents. It was an obvious but difficult choice. From the beginning I was able to encourage him even though I knew how much I would miss him. It just seemed so right for him, like a gift from God, that I trusted it would somehow be right for me as well. What was blessing for him would be blessing for me and for the community. He had a couple of months to live with the idea before the actual move took place. During that time, in mid-May, I went to the hermitage for my annual eight days of solitude. Byron came almost every day to celebrate mass with me. He needed to be constantly reassured that he was doing the right thing in leaving the community. I suggested that he consider it as a trial period of two months. If, at the end of that time, he felt it was not working, then he would be welcome to return to the Farm House.

On the night of May 31, I helped him complete his packing. Then we sat in the sunroom and played a few games of crib, with neither one of us having any interest in whether we won or lost. At noon the next day he went to a meeting at York Haven to sign the lease and pick up the keys to his apartment. In the late afternoon we packed all his belongings into his pickup truck. There were only a few of us home at the Farm House for a quick supper. Byron could hardly eat a thing. Then the two of us sat for a few moments in the sunroom while he had a coffee and smoked a cigarette. When he was finished he put his head in his hands and cried, "What am I getting myself into?" I did my best to reassure him. Then we drove across the city to his new home.

Along with Christine there were a couple of people from the Farm Community there at York Haven to help Byron get moved in. One of these was Damaso, a refugee claimant from Latin America who had spent some time with us and was returning for a visit. I had just picked him up at the bus station on my way to York Haven. Once almost everything was done I drove Damaso to the Farm House and saw that he got settled and had something to eat. Then I returned to Byron's apartment, where he was now alone. I took particular care in installing his telephone. We did a bit more arranging of his things, and then I put some ointment in his eyes, something that needed to be done nightly and was always easier if done by someone else.

Looking out the window I could see the Guelph Correctional Centre just across the road, the very place where this particular chapter of his life had begun 12 years earlier. On this first day of June 1992, Byron had just completed a very significant life circle. He seemed to be at peace as he climbed into bed and said his familiar "Good night, Pal." As I said good night and started to leave, I thought of his expression "Never go into a small town crying." The phrase took on a different meaning, even though this new home of his was not exactly a small town. He had his cry before leaving the Farm House, but he arrived here and settled in peacefully without a tear, ready to make the best of it. Driving back to the Farm House was my time for a good cry.

Six days later I went to York Haven to celebrate mass and ask for God's blessing on this new home and all who were living there. Christine had everything perfectly organized for the celebration with maximum participation of the residents. Even people who could hardly read were given the opportunity to do so and were made to feel supported as they struggled through it. People who couldn't read at all had the opportunity to bring forward the gifts of bread and wine or light the candles or perform some other task that made them feel part of the service. During the snacks afterwards we watched the video replay of the service to squeals of delight when people saw themselves involved in a way that they had never been in a regular church worship service. Afterwards, visiting with Byron in his apartment, I felt very good sensing how clearly he was fitting into this place and how much he had to offer by way of building community among the other residents. We had many good visits back and forth and kept in touch by phone. It quickly became clear that this had been a good move for Byron and that he was going to manage it very well.

As he became more settled, I began to realize that an important chapter in my life and the life of the community had come to completion. Twelve years earlier, when Martin Royackers was urging Doug McCarthy to accept Byron into the Farm Community, Doug had had strong reservations, concerned that "we could never handle that guy." Doug was almost right in this initial assessment but was relieved and grateful that we were able to handle that guy, who in fact turned out to be a real blessing to the community. So, with Byron settling into his new home, I was now freer to give more attention to the rest of the community, but also to myself and my own needs. I soon realized that in order to continue to be present to the community in a healthy way I needed to take some sabbatical time. I was now free to plan for this.

The plan that took shape was to give myself six months for rest and inner renewal beginning in January 1993. Early in that time I would spend a month of solitude in the Bahamas. There the Grey Nuns of Pembroke, Ontario, operated a school and mission on the sparsely populated island of Eluthera. They were offering me hospitality in a little guest house next to the church and rectory, where if I chose I could be of some assistance to the parish priest. Then, I would return briefly to Guelph before going to l'Arche in France for about ten weeks to bathe in that healing environment of friendship and prayer. My brother Gord had agreed to visit me there in Trosly and then join me on a trip to Africa. We would be spending time with a Jesuit classmate of mine, Fr. Jack Doyle, who had been in Zambia for 25 years. Jack was planning a trip to Zimbabwe that would take us past Victoria Falls and the nearby Kariba dam and hydro-electric power station, something that greatly interested Gord, a mechanical engineer who had recently retired from Ontario Hydro. I was delighted by the prospect of having this time with my brother. In all my adult life this would be the first extended time spent with any of my siblings.

* * * * *

MEANWHILE, BACK AT THE RANCH

December 19, 1985

Dear Mum and Dad,

It snowed today. To see it on the farm buildings and on the ploughed fields stirred some ancient memory that was very beautiful. We are putting up snow fences, and busy in the barn with the cattle – there are over 200 of them in the barns.

The most wonderful development in my life is that Jezebel the farm dog was banished from the main part of the farm, so she is now mine and lives here. There's a retreat house over there where nuns and priests come for 40-day silent retreats. They wander around on the land in deep contemplation, and Jezebel, who is an Australian Blue Heeler and is supposed to round up cattle by darting hither and thither nipping at their heels, finds it more fun and possibly safer to nip the heels of the nuns and priests on retreat. The other thing that people complained about was that when she greeted them she sometimes jumped up and bit their noses.

She's never been trained; she just spends her time leaping through the air like a kangaroo. She surprises small mice and voles that way, and crickets in summer. She sleeps in our barn now, and I am training her. This gives me a wonderful excuse to go out and be alone for a while every day in the fields or in the cedar bush. In only four days she is walking to heel without a lead. She always comes when you call, usually out of love but sometimes out of politeness.

Mary, our "Russian Princess," keeps coming in and telling me funny lines from the movie she is watching.

229

Byron went on a drunk this weekend. He kept dreaming about his family and finally something snapped and he went out and got himself a bottle of whisky. He's only just beginning to recover, because the pills he takes for alcoholism make him violently sick if he drinks. It is so hard, so unfair that the people who are already down get beaten down further.

New Year's Day 1986

This morning we had mass in the barn with the cows. It's a New Year's Day tradition: we all sit around on the steps up to the hayloft and on bales of hay, and try to become aware of the discomfort and poverty of where and how Jesus was born. The smell of manure and the drafts, for example. My bum nearly froze off. I'd take my gloves off to play the guitar and then shove them back on again. There were about 50 of us there, with the extended community, and then the cows, who rattled their stanchions as they watched us. If you don't know what a stanchion is, it's a sort of handcuff for a cow's neck.

Eileen, the volunteer from Newfoundland, and Pat, a Jesuit scholastic who lives here, have fallen madly in love. Eileen used to say of attractive young Jesuits, "You can look at the menu, but you can't buy." But this time she certainly seems to have bought.

Another of my favourite expressions of Eileen's is: "What you lose in the Our Fathers, you make up for in the Hail Marys, and what you lose in the Hail Marys, you make up for in the Our Fathers." It's astonishing how often it comes in handy.

Lots of love,

Weesa

16

Gone Fishing

I was so happy to see Byron after my three months' journey to l'Arche in France and to Zambia with my brother Gord. It was like coming home to another brother. Visiting with him in his apartment at York Haven, I was amazed and delighted to discover that, with the help of the patch, he had been off cigarettes for two months. This was no small miracle. We played a few games of cribbage and planned a fishing trip for the following week. Remembering our tearful goodbyes of a year earlier and how we had both dreaded the separation, I was deeply thankful that all had turned out so well. Having his own bachelor apartment spared Byron the stress of the ever-changing population of the Farm Community. Sr. Christine assured some continuity with his previous community and was a great support to him. For my part, I would not have been free to leave on a sabbatical if Byron had still been with us.

Thus it was that Byron picked me up at the Farm House at 8 a.m. on June 1, 1993 – one year to the day since he moved out. We stopped at Tim Horton's, hoping we might run into our local doctor so that I could get some more antibiotics for my cough that was dragging on. The doctor was not there but Byron got a coffee and we proceeded to his apartment. He had trouble locating his fishing gear. After that he continued wandering around like a goldfish in a bowl, looking for I don't know what. Finally, I just put his shaving kit, pyjamas and a few things he might need into his bag and guided him out the door and into his pickup truck. Then, with Byron at the wheel, we were on the road again, heading for Mary Grove (the vacation property of the Sisters of St. Joseph of Hamilton) on Lake Joseph in Muskoka. He drove more slowly and less confidently than usual and made a couple of wrong turns. After about 45 minutes I took over and drove the rest of the way. Byron had endless trucking stories to tell as we drove. The area triggered many memories in him, like the time he drove his rig with a 30-ton load of lumber the 40-plus kilometres up this same highway, from MacTier to Parry Sound, in the dead of night with no headlights, by tailgating a buddy of his in another truck. That was the same buddy, Frenchy, who in a slow line of trucks crossing the bridge at Cornwall had passing motorists turning their heads as he drove holding a newspaper stretched out in front of his face. They couldn't see the peep holes poked through it that allowed him to more or less see where he was going.

Shortly after 2 p.m. we arrived at Mary Grove. Our two-bedroom cottage was more than adequate for our needs. Byron did little to help us get settled in and quickly jumped into bed to sleep for a couple of hours. In the evening we watched Stanley Cup hockey: Montreal vs. Los Angeles.

The next day we took it easy. We fished from the dock for a while, catching and releasing a few small bass. In the late afternoon a mutual friend, Marie, from North Bay came by for a visit. I was shocked at how old Byron looked as he struggled to his feet to give her a hug. The three of us celebrated mass in the living room. Then, while Byron slept, the two of us cooked dinner: chicken, mashed potatoes and creamed corn. After Marie left, Byron and I fished from the dock for a short time, the water being too choppy for the boat. I caught and released a few small bass while Byron made one or two feeble casts then just let his line dangle over the edge of the dock until finally he lost interest altogether.

I went out in the boat for a while early the next morning as Byron continued to sleep. The stillness of the lake and the warmth of the morning sun were so peace-giving that I was grateful the fish weren't biting. In the afternoon we drove to Parry Sound. He showed me the jail where he spent seven months during the time of his trial. That's where he perfected his skill of killing flies with an elastic band and developed his love-hate relationship with "those damn seagulls" that came squawking to his cell window for breadcrumbs. Then Byron guided me to a mall in the north end of the city where he sent me into the drugstore to get him a nail brush to scrub the nicotine stains off his fingers. While I was doing this he went and bought cigarettes, removed the patch and started smoking. When I discovered him, I felt like a schoolteacher catching a child cheating on a test. We were both upset and disappointed and had to go to Tim Horton's for coffee and try to calm down. Before supper we celebrated mass at the kitchen table, a moment of much-needed peace. In the evening we watched another hockey game.

By the following day Byron was becoming more and more choked up with phlegm and having trouble getting it out, to the point where it was clouding his speech and ruining his appetite. That day we did no fishing. In the afternoon we drove to Bala with more trucking stories, as he remembered troubles he had had with a particular sharp curve or steep hill and getting a huge flatbed truck unstuck on the railway tracks just minutes before a train came through. Back at the cottage he was desperately trying not to smoke, putting on the patch, then a couple of hours later taking it off and having a smoke. Shaking his head as he stared at his cigarette he said mournfully, "This is what is going to kill me." He had pretty well won the battle against alcohol, which had almost killed him and others on more than one occasion, but he was losing it with nicotine. We celebrated mass in the evening after supper, remembering the 27th anniversary of my ordination to the priesthood. Then we played a few hands of cribbage. There was no fun in beating him since he didn't have his usual competitive spirit and couldn't seem to concentrate.

On day five, as Byron again slept late, I went out in the boat for a while, catching nothing but relishing the stillness and beauty of the morning. Later we had more conflict over cigarettes, with me refusing to go to the store and buy them for him. Finally, he went on his own. In the afternoon we drove to Port Carling. We got a druggist to contact Byron's doctor in Guelph for a prescription for antibiotics. Then we sat on the hill in front of the bakery having a coffee and soaking in the afternoon sun and the view, both of us kind of numb and hardly saying a word for almost an hour. Back at the cabin, Byron slept for an hour as I prepared a meatloaf for supper. After celebrating mass we, or rather I, fished for a very short time. Byron sat on the dock in the lawn chair I brought down for him, but he soon found the wind too cool. Back in the cottage we played a bit of cribbage as we watched the hockey game.

On Sunday we both slept late, and then in the early afternoon celebrated mass. Afterwards, while we were still sitting at the kitchen table, Byron said, "It has been really good to be able to have mass every day; it didn't always mean that much to me, but now it does." We had another discussion about his smoking, this time more peacefully. I told him that he might as well stop tormenting himself for now. Maybe later he could try again to stop. Then I went and bought cigarettes. That evening, having no desire for cribbage, we watched the video *Field of Dreams*.

That night I slept poorly and the next morning was up early. Byron got up much later, more congested than ever. The coffee I made sat in front of him getting cold until he ended up spilling it all. He started puffing on his lighter as though it were a cigarette, and then almost burned his face trying to light a cigarette he didn't have in his hand. Then he asked me, "What time did they come home last night?" When I asked who he meant, he said, "My wife and three daughters and sister-in-law." It wasn't long before he was back in bed without either a coffee or a cigarette. He slept most of the day. The few moments he was up he continued to be very confused. This was a terrible time for me. As the day progressed I became more and more worried, with no idea what to do. The weather was beautiful but I was afraid to go out and leave Byron alone. To distract myself I began reading James Mitchener's *Caribbean* as I sat on the back porch in the sun. I went fishing for half an hour and caught a good-sized bass. In the middle of the afternoon I finally got through to one of Byron's doctors. He suggested that Byron may not be getting enough oxygen to the brain because of his congestion. I didn't pick up any sense of urgency, as he suggested that I could get Byron checked out at Emergency. I began to clean up and pack, getting ready to return to Guelph, but I couldn't get Byron moving. Finally, around 6:30 in the evening, I convinced him to let me take him to Emergency. As we drove to Parry Sound, Byron desperately pleaded for a cigarette. Reluctantly I lit one for him, which he really didn't smoke. Then I lit a second one for him, which he clearly couldn't smoke.

After being quickly admitted into the hospital, Byron was put on a monitor, which showed his oxygen level to be very low. When the doctor called me over and asked me if my friend had ever made known his wishes with regards to life support, I felt as though I'd been kicked in the stomach. I had no idea that his condition was so serious. She explained to me that Byron might have to be put on a respirator to be kept alive.

Given his condition he might have to stay on it if he couldn't breathe on his own. At my suggestion, we both spoke with Byron about this but he had trouble grasping what the doctor was saying. Speaking alone with him, I was able to get the message through. He showed no sign of being upset and made his desire perfectly clear. Shaking his head he mumbled, "No machines, no machines." About 9 p.m. I called Sr. Christine, who said she would come as soon as possible. All during this time in the hospital, Byron was very kind and patient with the nurses and other staff, unlike the "Tiger" he was known as during other hospitalizations.

When Heather, the nurse from Intensive Care, took over, she gave me a sense of security and peace, allowing me to help her wheel Byron up to ICU and get him settled. By 1:30 a.m. he was sleeping and his condition seemed stable. Heather brought in a stretch-out chair so that I could spend the night next to my friend. Christine and Ed, a mutual friend, arrived about 2:30 am. Since Byron was sleeping and his oxygen level was higher and stable, it seemed all right to leave him, although I might have detected some disappointment in Heather as I told her we were going and would be back by 8 a.m. Christine, Ed and I drove back to Mary Grove and got to bed sometime after three.

All three of us were up and in the kitchen by 6:30 a.m., so at Christine's suggestion we set out for the hospital earlier than planned. When we entered the ICU, Heather said, "I'm so glad you're here; in the last hour Byron has not been responding, but maybe he will respond to you." The oxygen monitor was down to 34 from last night's high of 80, even lower than the 45 it had registered when he first arrived. He looked ghostly. Christine and I both greeted him: "Byron, it's me, Christine"; "Byron, it's me, Bill." At the sound of our names there was a flicker of recognition in his face. Heather asked me again about life support, and while I was trying to respond to her, Byron stopped breathing. A moment of terrible stillness and waiting. He did not take another breath. Christine, Ed and I were stunned. I looked at the clock. It was 7:30. I kept hoping and silently trying to urge Byron to take another breath. Just at that moment the doctor (the same, kind, pregnant woman from last night) came in. She confirmed that Byron had gone. While we were talking, a gasp came from his body, sparking an instant of hope, but the doctor said it was just the gases escaping. This happened a couple more times; each time a shudder ran through me. After a few minutes beside his bed, me on the right side, Christine on the left and Ed at the foot, I began to feel faint and had to sit down. Heather brought us some tea. The doctor reappeared and asked if we had any questions. She encouraged us to stay until she could return in about half an hour. Finally, we let the tears flow, embraced and tried to console each another. We said a few prayers as the reality began to set in that Byron was really gone.

I thanked Heather for all her kindness as she went off duty. The new nurse explained about signing the certificate of release for the undertaker and other practical details. The doctor, when she returned, spoke to us about the complications of Byron's condition and gave the cause of death as respiratory failure. Christine told her how Byron had been losing weight in recent months even though he was eating well. The doctor suggested that there probably was a recurrence of the cancer, and that in fact he looked to her like someone who had cancer. Her kindness was comforting.

I called a funeral home in Guelph. Later, remembering one of Byron's remarks – "You get a discount from the undertaker if you walk in" – I thought how disappointed he would be, missing out on this discount.

We left the hospital around 8:30 to return to Mary Grove. I shed some tears on the way driving alone in Byron's truck. While Christine and Ed cleaned up and packed, I made some phone calls to the community and other friends. Christine and Ed left and I stayed on for a while, making some more phone calls and trying to absorb what had happened.

Finally, I began the long, lonely ride home. As I drove I was at times flooded with gentle tears and occasionally with loud sobbing, along with images from this past week and memories from the past years. I realized that my constant prayer that Byron not die a violent death had been answered. He went so peacefully home to God, and for this I gave thanks. I also gave thanks for the miracle of those two months that he managed to stop smoking, since certainly it was that respite that kept him alive until my return from France. The prayer of St. Ignatius gave me some comfort: "Take, Lord, and receive all my liberty, my memory, my understanding, and my entire will, all that I have and possess. You have given all to me; to you, Lord, I return it. All is yours; do with it what you will. Give me only your love and your grace, that is enough for me."

Thank you, Byron, for these 13 years of friendship. It has been an amazing journey. We've been over some rough roads, we've made it around some tight curves, we've gone up some steep hills and down some breathtaking slopes, we've driven in bright sunlight and through dark nights and dense fog, and what a wild and wonderful ride it has been. Thanks for the ride, Pal, thanks for the ride.

* * * * *

MEANWHILE, BACK AT THE RANCH

Dear Mum and Dad,

I am really grateful for the 30-day retreat. It has left me in a positive frame of mind and confident that – that what? That Jesus loves me, that God is merciful, that goodness will triumph, has triumphed, over evil. I was chronically depressed and just not able to get out, but I knew that leaving the Farm Community was not the answer. If you can't have faith and hope right here and now, how can they be real? In fact it is in the most painful and sinful and darkest places of our lives that we meet God. The sharing after the retreat was incredible. The pain of people seeing that they have been living out of some false value and then the joy of rediscovering the source of who they are, the true love and the true meaning of their lives – especially if it is a priest or nun who has dedicated themselves to that, and may have totally lost touch with why – is one of the most moving things I have ever heard.

Lots of love,
Weesa

17

On the Road Again

Flanked and overshadowed by a pair of tall, wiry priests, all of us in white liturgical vestments, I walked up the aisle of the chapel of the funeral home towards the simple wooden casket that enclosed Byron's mortal remains. The chapel was filled to overflowing and, to organ accompaniment, all were singing "Amazing Grace." By the time the song had ended, we three priests had walked past the casket and turned to face it and the congregation.

In the awesome silence that followed the opening song I summoned all my courage, took a deep breath and began to speak. Although I was a stranger to few if any of the people there, I introduced myself by explaining that I had been a member of the Farm Community for 13 years, and that for 12 of those I had had the privilege of sharing a room with Byron. I added, "It wasn't always fun, but we managed." There was some modest laughter in response. Then I introduced my two companions.

To my left is Fr. Martin Royackers SJ, who has been a member of the Farm Community for the past four years and also for several months during an earlier period. This is the man who introduced Byron to the community. Martin used to

241

play crib with him when Byron was residing in a nearby institution. Byron told me how angry Martin would get whenever he lost. [Laughter] Now, I'm not saying that Martin lost often, only that he lost badly. [More laughter.]

To my right is Fr. Doug McCarthy SJ, the founder of the Farm Community, who was the director when Byron joined us. Doug and Byron by coincidence or providence happened to be from the same part of New Brunswick. Byron, who knew Doug's family and the street where he grew up, used to say, "The farther down that street you went the tougher they got…and McCarthy lived in the last house." [A roar of laughter] We all know that Byron had a great sense of humour, so we will have to laugh a little today as well as cry a little.

It was a relief for me to be actually doing this service, the thought of which had always filled me with dread.

On Tuesday, the day Byron died, I got back to the Farm House in the late afternoon. The folks there were very gentle and supportive to me, even though half of them had been welcomed while I was away on my sabbatical and hardly knew me or Byron. I was especially grateful that evening to have time on the phone with Christine, who was able to quickly see what needed to be done in terms of the wake and funeral. Fr. Martin, who was living at the Red House, was also very supportive. Fr. Doug was away in Calgary directing a retreat, but thought he could get back by Thursday night. It was reassuring to know that they would both be able to concelebrate the funeral mass with me on Friday.

Among the many people I called that night was the friend in the north who was in touch with Byron's family. The next day, when his oldest daughter called, my heart went out to her. That family had lived so much pain and fear, so much hurt with their father, and had had none of my experience of him during these years of redemptive transformation. I encouraged her to come for the funeral, assuring her of how welcome she and her sisters and mother would be. The mother and youngest daughter, she told me, were now in another part of the country and certainly would not be coming. For her part she was still unsure. I strongly hoped she would, and called the next day to further encourage her, but she was already on her way.

When I got to the funeral parlour on Thursday at two in the afternoon, Christine was already there with Ed and several people from Welcome In and York Haven. The casket, as we had decided earlier, was closed. It was surrounded by many bouquets of flowers from family and friends. On top of the casket were two large cards that had been made and signed by people from Welcome In and York Haven. Also, Christine had displayed there the framed enlargement of the photo I had taken of Byron and me each proudly holding up the big fish we had brought home from our first expedition to Owen Sound. Along with the photo was a framed copy of the doggerel poem I had written for one of Byron's birthdays:

Happy Birthday to a Fine Man and a Good Friend

He came to the Farm House two years ago.
Why did he come, you'd like to know.
His answer to this straight out would pop
With a twinkle of the eye, "Are you a cop?"

So now you know of whom I speak:
Our dear friend, Byron, the man of the week.

'Twas on March 13 that he came to be
In Chatham, New Brunswick, by the Miramichi.
And on March 19 two years ago
He joined our community, as you all know.

So these are the dates we like to measure
Since they brought to life and to us this priceless treasure.

Byron may be Dunn but he's just begun
To fill our lives with wisdom and fun,
As he tells us tales from out of the past
And speaks of things that are deep and vast.

He's great on a tractor – ploughs real straight rows
Except when he sometimes happens to doze.
But it's in the saddle that he really picks up
And rides the range like Wild Bill Hickup.

Byron Dunn, he's the one and only
Who keeps my life from being too lonely.

For we share a room, which I must confess
Is sometimes in an awful mess
But it's home to him and it's home to me
And I'm deeply grateful as you can see.

We have interesting times in our little room;
Sleepwalking and talking with a bang and a boom.
But I wouldn't change it and I hope it doesn't end
For I've got myself a real fine friend.

So I thank you, Byron, without impunity
For all that you bring to this community.
And I pray that your years ahead will be blessed
Since you really deserve the very best.

Now you may be wondering who wrote this mess
But "does Eaton's tell Simpson's all its business?"

I recognized Byron's two brothers and their wives, since they had maintained contact with him and occasionally came to the Farm House. The younger brother and his wife had come all the way from Alberta, where Byron had visited them for a week about six years earlier. All of them appeared uneasy and distraught but spoke to me with kind appreciation.

Many people came to the afternoon visitation and even more in the evening, including Byron's two older daughters with their husbands. I was deeply moved to finally meet these fine women, and along with Christine did my best to welcome and comfort them. I can only imagine how difficult it must have been for them to be there.

Several of Byron's uncles and aunts and a nephew were also there. They may have known Byron in his somewhat better younger days, before the alcohol had completely taken hold of him, but they had not had the privilege the majority of us there had of knowing the older, wiser Byron growing in gentleness, kindness and patience. We were freer to shed tears and to be more joyful during the wake, telling the stories of him that many of us knew but could never hear often enough.

Later that night I found it comforting to be with my fellow Jesuits, Doug and Martin, to plan the funeral service, and have them take over all the practical details involved. Just knowing that the two of them, who knew and loved Byron as much as they did, would be at my side made it possible to trust that all would go well.

After I had completed the welcome and introductory prayer at the funeral, a woman from York Haven known as Little Maria came forward and read a poem. Her unclear speech and limited reading ability made it difficult to understand, but the poem had something nicely sentimental to say about the enduring nature of friendship. When she had finished reading she spoke in a soft voice: "Byron was my buddy...we had long talks...we used to joke a lot…but most of all he needed a little cuddle now and then."

Sheila, a woman who clearly had her own sufferings in life and who had been welcomed by Christine onto her team and into her apartment, read words of comfort and encouragement from one of St. Paul's letters. Weesa and Val, both playing guitars, sang a plaintive duet, "The Lord Is My Shepherd."

Mary the Russian Princess read the alleluia verse, "The stone which the builders rejected has become the chief cornerstone." Mary and Byron had become friends while living together in the Farm House. Byron had been especially patient and gentle with Mary during the difficult year in which she went through a breakdown that saw her become emotionally out of control with terrible outbursts of anger, until finally it seemed best to her and to us that she live in a more structured environment. After she moved to the new facility, Byron faithfully picked her up every Friday and took her out for a coffee or for lunch. Even today, Mary continues to be grateful for his kindness to her, and to remember joyfully his funny stories and great sense of humour.

As a gospel text for my sermon I chose John 20:19-30 about the Easter event when, the doors being closed for fear of the authorities, Jesus appears in the midst of the disciples and says, "Peace be with you," then shows them his hands and his side and missions them even as he had been missioned by the Father. This text also includes the part about Thomas who, having missed this appearance, insists that he will not believe unless he touches the wounds in Jesus' hands and side, and how eight days later Jesus shows up in the same way as before and obliges Thomas to do just that.

I began by saying, "I chose this text because it speaks to us about wounds and about joy and resurrection, life beyond suffering and death." I was conscious of the importance of honouring the pain and hurt of his family as well as the goodness and joy in Byron that many of us had experienced. It also seemed important to try to free his family from any false sense of guilt they might have. I went on to speak of how Jesus came to those faithless disciples who had abandoned him in his hour of need, and the first thing he said to them was "Peace be with you," without a single inference of condemnation. Then, confidently, he commissioned them to continue his mission of forgiveness.

Next, I referred to what I considered to be the prophetic words of Thomas: "unless I touch his wounds I will not believe." I spoke of these as being words of faith rather than of doubt, implying that we must be in touch with the wounds of others and our own wounds if we are to find meaning and life.

Our friend, brother, relative Byron had many wounds. Due to that terrible accident his face was badly marred, a wound that was very visible, but he also had deeper wounds in his psyche and in his heart. Yet in some ways these wounds, like those of Jesus, became signs of victory rather than defeat. That is the amazing aspect of this story in John's Gospel: Jesus, to show that he was risen, didn't say *Look how fantastic I am, see how I can pass through locked doors*, or *See how radiant I am and how beautiful my garments are*. He said to Thomas, "Touch my wounds and doubt not longer but believe." His wounds are now glorious signs of victory, signs of resurrection. Those of us who have been touched by Byron over these past 13 years know that Byron lived a kind of resurrection through those wounds…with much pain and much struggle but with his incredible courage to go on and that great sense of humour that never left him.

Byron was a truck driver, as we all know. Truck drivers don't have a lot of room for feelings and emotions. Truck drivers have to get from point A to point B as fast as possible. So Byron drove hard. He was a tough man. He was a scrapper. The family know that well. [Christine had seen to it that the family not be obliged to sit in the front pews, and they gratefully accepted to sit towards the rear, mingled in with everyone else.] Byron told me that when he was a boy his father instructed him to hit first and ask questions later. His brothers know that all too well. For him fighting was a way of life…and he fought for life. I never knew him to be intentionally mean. But he did have a terrible temper and the power alcohol had over him at times made him crazy. Gradually in these last years, these resurrection years, it was beautiful to see how he fought to overcome the hold that alcohol had on him and that terrible temper that had caused him so much suffering and so much suffering for others. And he triumphed.

We know him mostly as a man with a fantastic personality and a magnificent sense of humour and a great awareness and attentiveness to people.

In the 12 years that we shared that room together in the Farm House, just north of here, there were many, many people who came through that house, and in a way Byron was the guestmaster. He welcomed people so attentively and so lovingly, and if you met him once you could never forget him. That is why this chapel is filled to overflowing.

When I phoned Don and Elinor to tell them the news, their son, Dustin, just a boy but nevertheless a young man of wisdom, said that it is good that Byron died doing what he liked to do. Yes, Byron died while we were on a fishing trip. We weren't actually fishing at the time, but we had fished a little, and caught a few fish, of course. Last night at the wake I was standing in front of that picture of Byron and me with the big salmon, and Nelson said to me; "Did you guys really catch those fish, or did you buy them? Now remember you're a priest so you have to tell the truth." I told Nelson, "Yes, as a priest I need to tell the truth, but as a fisherman…as a fisherman I have to tell a good story."

At that point I resumed for the congregation the story of Byron's last hours, underlining how gentle and grateful he was with the nurses and how even in his weakness at the point of death he did not lose his sense of humour. This, I concluded, is the true story — told by the priest.

Now if Byron were here — well, he is here, but he's not talking — but if Byron were telling the story it might go something like this: "While Bill and I were fishing, I hooked into a huge fish, it was so big that it pulled me off the dock and into the lake but I wasn't going to let go of such a great catch. Well, the fish was pulling me all around the lake and when it pulled me by the dock again Bill had the net ready to save me but I hollered never mind me, save the fish."

He was a storyteller, as we all know, and he loved the north. So it was fitting that he died in the north, in Parry Sound, close to where he had lived with his family, a place where he experienced many good times as well as a great deal of pain. In every little town we went through in that area he had a story to tell — mostly trucking stories. He was a storyteller and his stories were always fascinating.

Now, the final story is that this man, struggling through life, fought against his anger and he won. He became gentle, he became very gentle, and in one way or another he has touched us all. Some who knew more of his anger were frightened by his anger, and well they should have been. But ultimately he wished no harm to anyone. A few times he wished harm to himself because he was afraid of what his anger could do to others. It always struck me after an outburst of anger how upset he would be with himself. He did not wear it lightly, that anger of his, and he suffered with it.

Now, as I say, Jesus himself wore these scars even after he rose from the dead. Byron certainly had his scars. His face was badly scarred. But gradually he became more accepting of his scars. There are some interesting stories about that nose he wore attached to his glasses. [Everyone had a good laugh when I told the story about Byron complaining to the police officer that he had lost his nose.]

We all have many stories we could tell about Byron, and I hope that in the coming days we can continue to share these with one another, but what is obvious to all of us is that this was an extraordinary man who has touched our lives deeply, and whose memory we will cherish. Jesus shines through the faces of each one of us. He shone through the face of Byron even in his wounds. So Byron's life challenges us to see the face of God in everyone we meet.

He was not a churchy man, but in his own way he was a religious man. In those last few days together up at the camp where we were staying we had mass every day either in the living room or at the kitchen table. Last Sunday when we finished he said to me, "You know, it's so good to have mass every day...it didn't always mean that much to me...there were times when I didn't need it or want it, but I do now." Deeply he was religious, and he saw beauty in the faces of people and he loved them. Even if he was out of touch with them, his love was faithful, for his family and for his friends. So as we hear this gospel of Jesus who suffered and died and who rose triumphantly, no longer ashamed of his wounds but bearing them as a sign of victory, we can think of the Jesus who has been revealed to us in Byron Dunn, who has revealed to us beauty and love and courage and fidelity. We have much to be grateful for and we have treasured memories that will continue to carry us through the years...thank God.

As we came to the end of the service, Weesa and Val led the congregation in singing "Swing Low, Sweet Chariot." Then Fr. Martin said the final prayers of blessing and farewell over the casket. Almost everyone from the funeral service came in the cortege the few blocks through the city and the equivalent of another block beyond the city to Resurrection Cemetery, which borders our farm. I drove in the lead car with Ed and Jody, a young man from York Haven to whom Byron had been especially kind.

Arriving at the gravesite I was thrilled to see its location: almost on the highest point of the cemetery land and just a few feet from our property line, a few feet from one of the hayfields that in springs gone by Byron would have ploughed and harrowed and from which in summer heat and dust he would have driven wagonloads of hay. It was like bringing his body home. New Brunswick had once been home for him, but this he chose to leave in order to grow up. The near north of Ontario had been home for him, but this he destroyed in alcoholic rage and confusion. On this farm he came home not just from another long road trip to rest and drink before heading out again, but home where he could finally end the roaring and racing down life's highway. Here is where he came home to himself, and in the process helped me to come home to myself as well. Here we both found a home for our hearts. I was happy to know that I would only have to walk across a few fields to visit his final resting place. Here I could come in times of doubt to be assured by his words of wisdom: *Up the road and down the road* and *If things don't change they're going to stay the way they are* and other priceless gems.

Fr. Doug and Christine led the prayers at the graveside. Just before the casket was lowered into the ground, the undertaker removed from the top of it the metal crucifix and handed it to me. This crucifix at Catholic burials is traditionally handed to the closest next of kin in attendance. It did not seem right to me that I should be the one to have this memento, so I turned and offered it to Byron's daughter, who was standing just behind me. She gave me a look of uncertainty and maybe even fear, but after a reassuring glance from her husband she accepted it. Finally, Doug invited those who wished to do so to throw a handful of earth onto the casket before leaving, and encouraged everyone to come to the reception at Ignatius College, which was just the other side of the narrow strip of hayfield.

The handful of dry earth that I dropped into the grave clattered on the casket with a sound of terrible finality, but it evoked in me feelings of gratitude as well as sadness. A long journey had ended, and a mysterious new one was beginning.

What would his be like now? What would mine be like without him?

The only memory I have of the reception is one that I cherish dearly: Byron's daughter saying to me, "Thank you — you really knew my father."

For the next couple of weeks I walked almost every stretch of our 600 acres looking at the rocks. While doing this I was slowly integrating the pain of having just buried my dearest friend and the almost joyful privilege of having been the priest who led the worship service of thanksgiving for his life and blessing for his final journey. When, a year earlier, another dear friend, Henry, whom I had known for over 35 years, died suddenly, I found that I needed to focus all my energies on trying to comfort and support his family. There was no space for me to do my own grieving. However, with Byron, even though I was the priest leading the burial service, I was supported by present and former members of the Farm Community and many others who understood my loss and gave me the space and encouragement to grieve. In this process, I discovered that I was grieving not only for Byron but also for Henry and many other losses of my life. So this searching on the land was a gentle, healing time for me.

Finally, I found what I was looking for, the right stone: greyish-white granite flecked with darker grey, about two feet long, a foot high and maybe 10 inches deep. It was down in a gully near some old ruins. Since it was too heavy for me to lift, it took mammoth determination and half an hour of straining and sweating to roll it to the top of the steep incline then slide it up a two-by-ten plank onto the tailgate of the truck that had been willed to me but would always be "Byron's truck." At the farm workshop I cleaned the stone with wire brushes and buffing tools. Then Ed and I installed it on the grave after he had fastened to it the plaque he had made: BYRON DUNN, "On the Road Again."

Many years earlier, during the time that I spent in the Novitiate less than a hundred yards from Byron's grave, I often heard the catchphrase spoken by older Jesuits to those in formation: "Courage and perseverance!" In those early days I had no idea just how much these two virtues would be needed over the long haul, especially during these recent years. Nor did I have any idea just how rich and fulfilling the journey would be. Not in my wildest dreams could I have imagined that one of my greatest teachers of courage and perseverance would be an ex-convict who had done time for attempted murder, and that friendship with him would be such a rich source of joy and fulfillment. It makes me wonder how many other wisdom figures and friends I have ignored and missed along the way; but now at least I try to be a little more attentive.

I often come here to Byron's grave, especially when I feel the need for support and encouragement, remembering his courage and his fun-loving spirit, knowing that he is still with me on the journey, delighting in the challenge of stormy weather or rough roads, and proclaiming with his muffled, raspy voice, "Don't back off, Bill. Don't back off."

Epilogue

November 4, 2003

Dear Bill,

After reading your book I couldn't stop walking around and around the house, overwhelmed by memories. It's now 10 years since Byron died, and nearly 20 since I arrived at the Farm Community. Can you believe that?

My daughter, Miriam, sits working on her math homework, my lifelong friend Don vacuums up an infestation of clusterflies, and another friend boils up a lamb bone for soup. I stop pacing to stick a log in the wood stove, which in itself moves me beyond all words at the remembrance of all we lived together.

I knew a lot of Byron's story, but there's a lot about you that I never knew. I don't blame you for not telling me at the time. Everyone else had their guts spread out over the table – someone had to keep them in the chicken. And as for what you and Byron were doing when you went off together, I wasn't interested at the time. I was only interested in when you were coming home and bringing the fish, but mostly the security, into our lives. Lucky I didn't know that your sense of being in control was about as solid as the fish stories were true.

It's hard to read some of the stuff in your book. I keep thinking of that line of Ignatius' prayer, "In thy wounds, hide me." We walked a thin and sometimes dangerous line between the almost fateful acceptance of pain, living as we did among people for whom it was an inevitable lifelong companion, and the human and necessary struggle to avoid or overcome it. You walked that line with Byron on a daily basis, sharing the experience of so many millions of people the world over struggling to live their faith beside addicted people whom they love. It makes you very vulnerable. I had to build up scar tissue to make the transition into the world again. I felt like I was in one of those dreams where you find yourself standing naked in the middle of a parking lot.

My life now may be different, but so much of it is an inheritance from my life with you and Byron, Tom, Liz, Mary and Wayne. Without a doubt the Farm Community was my formation, as you Jesuits say, and you were my role model. It didn't take too long to find out why some of the people had been "rejected by society." I found I had a lot of sympathy for society, such as when I spent hours one winter with a pick-axe chipping frozen silage off the silo walls because someone had been too lazy to fork it out properly. You listened patiently to me raging, and then turned me around and said, forgive, love, be grateful. Over and over again. It made me mad as hell.

At the Farm Community I learned how to fix a broken hay mower in mid-harvest, reverse a four-wheeled haywagon, build a set of mangers with a chainsaw, and round up a dozen escaped steers on a suburban lawn. I also learned not to be afraid of people who've been in psychiatric hospitals or prisons. I would have been terrified of such people in my former life. I learned not to be afraid of being marginalized myself. I learned that if I feel far from God, the surest way to get close again is to be close to marginalized people, whether they be poor, very old, very young, ill or crazy.

But I speak as if my own spiritual growth is the only thing that mattered. What about all the people who still need a Farm Community, but for whom it doesn't exist anymore? Who will be brave enough to give the visionaries of this world like Doug McCarthy the chance to act out such a radical Gospel vision? It won't come from state or political or for-profit institutions, and the religious communities are mostly dying. Where will my daughter get the chance to learn from working alongside wisely foolish people like you and Doug McCarthy, Christine Leyser and Martin Royackers?

Your book doesn't answer these questions. It is not an ecclesiological, theological or spiritual treatise, but it does celebrate friendship. At the Farm Community I made some lifelong friends, including you. We all lived something together – perhaps like war veterans – that will unite us forever. You and I don't have the chance to spend much time together these days, with me in Quebec City and you in Guelph, but remember when Wayne worked painstakingly for weeks in the sunporch on a paint-by-numbers version of the Last Supper? We have to trust that. One day we'll all be together again. We'll be all sitting around the Farm House table, Wayne's Last Supper on the wall behind us, a good fire in the stove and the Grey Cup game on the TV in the background, eating one of your magnificent Sunday lunch fry-ups.

Weesa